DR. FRED'S
WEATHER WATCH

OTHER SCIENCE ACTIVITY BOOKS BY McGRAW-HILL

Wacky Water Fun
by Ed Sobey

Fantastic Flying Fun
by Ed Sobey

SCIENCE FUNDAMENTALS SERIES:
FUNtastic Science Activities for Kids

Heat FUNdamentals

Light FUNamentals

Electricity and Magnetism FUNdamentals

Mechanics FUNdamentals

Sound FUNdamentals

by Robert W. Wood

Bouncing Eggs!
by William Wellnitz

DR. FRED'S WEATHER WATCH

How to Create and Run Your Own Weather Station

Fred Bortz, Ph.D.
with J. Marshall Shepherd, Ph.D.

McGraw-Hill

New York   San Francisco   Washington, D.C.
Auckland   Bogotá   Caracas   Lisbon   London   Madrid   Mexico City
Milan   Montreal   New Delhi   San Juan   Singapore   Sydney   Tokyo   Toronto

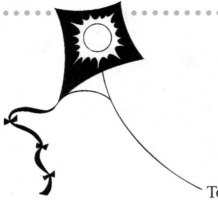

To Eliana and Elon,
May your lives be brightened with the sunshine of love.
May your minds be nourished by the gentle rain of wisdom.
May your courage be forged in the struggles of stormy days.
May your spirits soar on the breeze of *Shalom*.

McGraw-Hill

A Division of The **McGraw-Hill** Companies

pbk 1 2 3 4 5 6 7 8 9 0   DOC / DOC   0 9 8 7 6 5 4 3 2 1 0

ISBN 0-07-134799-2

Library of Congress Cataloging-in-Publication data applied for.

McGraw-Hill books are available at special quantity discounts to use as premiums and sales promotions. For more information, please write to the Director of Special Sales, Professional Publishing, McGraw-Hill, Two Penn Plaza, New York, NY 10121-2298. Or contact your local bookstore.

Acquisitions editor: Griffin Hansbury
Editing supervisor: Maureen B. Walker
Production supervisor: Charles Annis
Illustrations: Ingrid Olson <tulbox@earthlink.net>
Book design: Jaclyn J. Boone <bookdesign@rcn.com>

Printed and bound by R. R. Donnelley & Sons Company.

CONTENTS

PREFACE

WHO IS DR. FRED AND WHY DID HE WRITE THIS BOOK ?

Throughout the pages of this book, your guide will be a caricature called "Dr. Fred" — a cartoon character based on a real person named Dr. Alfred B. Bortz. Dr. Bortz has been a scientist all his life. From the time he was a child called "Fred" or "Freddie," he loved discovering the way the world works. He asked lots of questions. He quickly decided that what he liked best about questions is that they led to even more questions. Following one question to another is called research.

A scientist earns the title "doctor" by going to college, then studying a few years longer to become very good at research in a particular subject. That's what Dr. Bortz did. His subject was physics, the study of matter and energy. After college, he went to work, teaching math and physics or doing research for three universities and two companies for more than twenty years.

Although Dr. Alfred B. Bortz loved that work, young Fred kept pestering him, reminding him how much more fun science could be when shared with eager young readers. Finally, the serious Dr. Alfred B. Bortz stepped aside and let the friendly, enthusiastic Fred take over. He decided to call himself "Dr. Fred" to let his readers know that he was still very serious about science, but willing to be less serious about himself.

The "Dr. Fred" caricature looks and acts a lot like the real Dr. Fred. His love of questions and discovery show up in the question marks and exclamation points on his cap and the smile on his face. How much does he love questions and discovery? He loves them so much that he wouldn't write a book if he couldn't learn something along the way.

This book began with a discovery — not a scientific one, but a human one. Dr. Fred had an assignment to find and interview an "up-and-coming" young meteorologist (a person who studies the weather) for an article he was writing for people your age.

That meteorologist was J. Marshall Shepherd, who was working at NASA while completing his college research to earn the title of doctor for himself. By the time the interview was over, Dr. Fred had decided to write this book, with help from his new friend, Marshall Shepherd.

In that interview, Dr. Shepherd described how he got started in meteorology. As a sixth grader in North Canton, Georgia, about forty miles north of Atlanta, young Marshall watched and listened to weather predictions for the big city to the south, but he wanted to know what weather might be coming to his small town. He asked a research question, "Can I predict the weather for North Canton?" and set out to answer it as a science fair project.

He began by building his own weather station from inexpensive materials he found around the house. His simple instruments worked well enough for him to understand and predict his town's weather. He won first prize in his regional science fair and finished second in the Georgia State Science Fair! If you were doing the same project today, you would have much more information available than young Marshall did. You could buy an inexpensive weather forecasting kit. You could go to the World Wide Web and find detailed weather information for your exact location.

But would you learn any more than sixth-grader Marshall Shepherd did with his home made equipment? Probably not. In fact, by building the equipment as he did, you would probably come to understand the measurements and the weather better than any other way of learning it.

In this book, Dr. Fred will lead you along Marshall Shepherd's road to success. He will show you how to make and use instruments that measure the weather. You can buy the equipment that he teaches you how to build, but you will probably have more fun struggling to make your own. You can find weather forecasts for your area on the radio, television, or the World Wide Web, but you can have more fun trying to come up with your own. You may even become an expert forecaster for your neighborhood as Marshall Shepherd did for North Canton.

Then you will know why Dr. Fred wrote this book. He wrote it for everyone who wants to discover that the answer to Marshall Shepherd's research question is *"Absolutely yes!"* A young person can learn to predict the weather and can have a great time discovering how.

WORLD WIDE WEB   WEATHER WATCH

Dr. Fred's Weather Links   http://www.fredbortz.com/

INTRODUCTION
THE WEATHER AND YOU

What could be simpler than the Earth's atmosphere — the air we breathe? It has no color, no odor, no taste, and very little weight. Light passes through it almost unchanged. Almost all of it is within ten kilometers (about six miles) of our planet's surface. If Earth were as big around as a basketball, the atmosphere would be thinner than a sheet of paper.

But inside that thin layer can rage powerful storms. Clouds form and grow in hours, last for days, then disappear as ice, sleet, snow, or rain falling to the surface. Lightning flashes, thunder crashes, winds howl in ever-changing patterns. Even the sturdiest trees can be uprooted. Homes and buildings can be destroyed. Years of wind and rain, freezing and thawing, change solid rock into soft soil.

Despite its never-ending changes, this action in the atmosphere called weather can be predicted. We know that the energy for these awesome natural events comes from a single star, 150 million kilometers (93 million miles) away, the Sun. We understand that daily and yearly changes in the weather come from our planet's steady rotation on its tilted axis. We know that atmospheric conditions are affected by the masses of land and water on our planet's surface.

The scientific study of the weather, called meteorology, is as exciting and interesting as the weather itself. Unlike many scientists, who study things that most people have never heard of or experienced, meteorologists study something that affects everyone everyday. All meteorologists study the weather and many predict it. Their forecasts, though far from perfect, are usually reliable.

Today, nearly everyone makes decisions about what to do, where to go, and what to wear based on meteorological predictions. Farmers depend on weather forecasts to plan their planting and harvests. Pilots plan their routes to avoid powerful storms. Not many years ago, deadly and damaging hurricanes came ashore from the ocean almost without warning.

Today, with advanced computers, satellites, radars, and other new technologies, meteorologists can track severe storms from the start, giving people time to protect their property and themselves.

Many scientists use words that ordinary people don't understand, but the words of weather forecasters come into our living rooms daily. Thanks to radio and television, most people understand the words and know about the tools of meteorology. Those tools can be very fancy — television stations compete with advanced radar and satellite images and flashy computer-generated displays.

Still, weather forecasting begins with simple, basic measurements and historical weather record-keeping. Using mainly items you can find around the house, you can build simple instruments to make those same measurements in your neighborhood. Your back yard or school can become a weather station and the headquarters of your very own Neighborhood Weather Watch.

This book aims to help young people, teachers, and parents become amateur weather scientists. It explains how to gather and use information about the basic condition of the atmosphere, just as professional meteorologists do.

Through its pages and diagrams, you will learn to measure and record — using your own home-made weather station — air pressure, temperature, humidity (moisture in the air), wind speed, wind direction, and the amount of rainfall. You will learn how to recognize clues to the arrival of weather "fronts" and "systems." You will learn how to create and use a local weather record that will help you predict conditions to come.

The book also includes information about how you can find and use advanced measurements of our planet and atmosphere — the same data that professional meteorologists use to study the weather and create their forecasts. Then, using your home-made weather station, you can see how the atmospheric conditions of your small neighborhood fit into a fascinating world-wide pattern of ever-changing, yet often predictable, weather.

So open your eyes, roll up your sleeves, and let the fun begin!

CHAPTER 1

MEASURING THE WEATHER

Anyone who pays attention to weather reports knows the words for the measurements meteorologists use. Temperature, humidity, barometric pressure, wind speed and direction, precipitation (rain, snow, or sleet), visibility, and cloud conditions are all included in a typical weather report. Each of these measures something important about the weather.

Some of those measurements are easy to understand, because we feel them with our bodies or see them with our eyes. We can tell if the temperature is high or low by whether the air feels hot or cold. We can judge speed of the wind by feeling it blowing and watching what it moves. We can collect precipitation and know how deep the rain or melted snow would be if it just puddled on the ground.

We can feel humidity on hot days. "Relative humidity" tells how much water the air is holding compared to the maximum amount it could hold. When the air already has a lot of moisture in it, our perspiration does not evaporate easily. So we feel "sticky" and uncomfortable on hot, humid days. When the humidity is low, perspiration can evaporate easily. As it does so, it draws heat from our bodies, making us more comfortable even on a hot day.

We usually don't feel barometric pressure, but it is probably the most important weather measurement for forecasting. You'll learn more about it in the next chapter. The rest of this chapter will help you understand the basic rules for making measurements of the weather — or anything else.

Making Measurements

Let's start with the most common weather measurement, air temperature. If you live in the United States, you are probably accustomed to hearing temperatures in degrees Fahrenheit (devised by a German scientist with that last name). In most of the rest of the world, people use the Celsius scale, named for the Swedish scientist who proposed it.

Temperature measurements are written using the degree sign, a small raised circle ($^{\circ}$) followed by the capital letter F for Fahrenheit or C for Celsius. Water freezes at 0°C or 32°F and boils at 100°C or 212°F. The Fahrenheit scale is convenient for day-to-day living, since air temperature in most areas rarely goes above 100°F and rarely drops below 0°F. Scientists prefer the Celsius scale and its hundred-degree range of temperatures for liquid water. Celsius has also become the official temperature scale for weather reports in most countries.

The Celsius scale was formerly called centigrade, because there are one hundred (*centi* - in Latin) degrees (or gradations) between the normal freezing and boiling temperatures of water at sea level.

Your weather station will need a thermometer to measure air temperature in either Fahrenheit or Celsius degrees. You will also want to have a record book to keep track of temperature changes on an hour-to-hour or day-to-day basis. It doesn't matter which temperature scale you use as long as you are consistent, although many science fair judges prefer Celsius. Some science fairs even require temperatures to be measured in Celsius.

Like all measurement instruments, your thermometer will not be perfect. Scientists face that problem with every measurement they make.

Let's first discuss, then practice, the ways scientists deal with that. The *precision* of an instrument describes how small an amount it can measure. The *accuracy* of a measurement describes how confident you can be in it. Here's an example to help you understand precision and accuracy better. Suppose a creature from the planet Glorp arrives in a space ship and begins to measure the size of objects on Earth using a ruler made of a strange metal. You examine the ruler and find that it is marked in with lines separated by exactly one gleep, the basic Glorpian unit of length. You would then say that its precision is one gleep.

How accurate is that ruler? This exercise will help. Using the picture of the Glorpian ruler, make your own 180-gleep Glorpian tape measure from twelve 15-gleep paper strips taped together. Then use that tape measure to find the length and width of this page to the nearest gleep. Next measure other things, perhaps the height or waistline of some of your friends, to the nearest gleep.

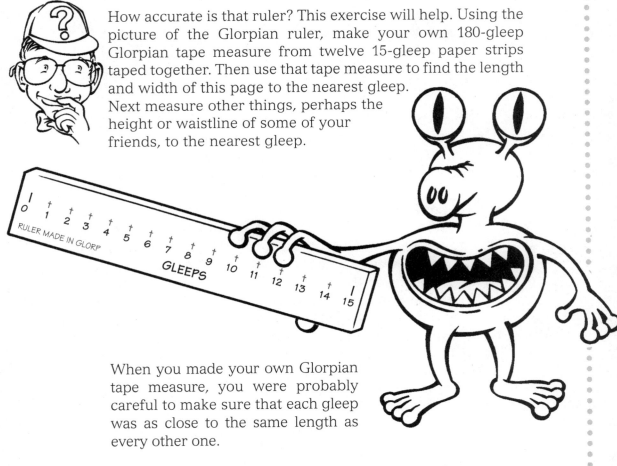

When you made your own Glorpian tape measure, you were probably careful to make sure that each gleep was as close to the same length as every other one.

You also did your best to make the length of the gleeps the same as those on the original ruler.

For instance, you may have made twelve copies of this page on a copy machine then cut out the copies of the ruler and carefully taped them together. Did you think about whether the copies are exactly the same size as the original. Couldn't they be a little bit larger or smaller, say by one part in a thousand? You'd never notice a difference that small, but it would make your 180-gleep tape measure inaccurate by that same amount. That's what we mean by accuracy — how close your measuring instrument comes to the actual value.

Even if the copies match the Glorpian ruler perfectly, it still might not give an accurate measurement in gleeps. The special Glorpian metal is probably like most metals here on Earth, so the ruler might get a little bit longer when it gets warmer. Then the spacings between its lines might be a little longer or smaller than when the spacecraft left Glorp

To check that, you decide to do an experiment on the Glorpian ruler. You raise its temperature $10^{o}C$ and carefully measure its length. It's longer by one part in a thousand! That ruler is not accurate unless the temperature on Glorp is the same as where you are.

"I wonder if the Glorpian astronaut thought of that?" you ask yourself. As if reading your mind, the creature scurries back into its spaceship, comes out with a thermometer, and sets it down beside the ruler. After waiting a few minutes the Glorpian reads the temperature, $46^{o}G$, then turns a knob on the end of the ruler. You watch in astonishment as the markings on the ruler shift a tiny bit. To keep the ruler accurate, the Glorpian adjusted it to match the new planet. That is called *calibration*. When you build your weather station, you will need to calibrate your measuring tools, too.

Interpreting and Understanding
Your Measurements

Making measurements is only the first step in becoming an expert weather watcher. You'll need to keep careful records. It is usually best to have a bound weather log-book to keep your records in one place. You will want to design your own charts, graphs, and forms for recording your measurements. Most scientists prefer to use a log-book with its pages ruled like graph paper. That gives them the flexibility to organize their records in many different arrangements or formats.

This book will suggest using different formats for different records. After a while, however, you may find that you prefer a different organization. That's fine, as long as the information is complete, accurate, and clear to anyone who wants to study it. As Dr. Fred's retired dentist used to tell him, "That's why they make chocolate and vanilla." Dr. Fred, never one to follow the usual paths, prefers butter pecan; but he doesn't skip dessert — and he always keeps a log of his important scientific measurements and observations.

After you take and record the measurements with your weather station for a while, you will begin to know your instruments well.

You will:
- know their precision and their limitations
- know how to calibrate them
- know how to observe, measure, and think like a scientist
- come up with ideas about relationships between your measurements and changes in the weather
- plan systematic measurements and observations to test those ideas
- become an expert at using your home-made instruments to measure and forecast the weather in your neighborhood.

Fortunately, you won't have to start your predictions "from scratch." To become a scientific forecaster, you will begin by learning about the weather research that came before you. In this book and in other places, you will read about what other scientists have already discovered. You will learn to apply the weather-forecasting principles they developed. Finally, you will begin to ask important questions about the weather in your own little corner of the world.

When that happens, you will be an expert weather watcher. That's Dr. Fred's forecast for your future!

CHAPTER 2
AIR PRESSURE

When you go for a medical check-up, the doctor takes many simple measurements to make sure your body is healthy. One of the simplest is your weight. You step on a scale, and it tells the doctor how many kilograms or pounds you weigh. The doctor marks that number on your chart, compares it to your previous measurements. The doctor also compares it to typical measurements for other young people of your age, sex, and height.

From that one measurement and the way it has been changing over your lifetime, the doctor cannot only get an idea of your general health but can also make predictions about your future. "You'll never play tackle for the Pittsburgh Steelers," the doctor correctly forecast for the lightweight son of the author.

The air around us has weight, too. For meteorologists, that weight — and the way it is changing — is one of the most important numbers for predicting the weather.

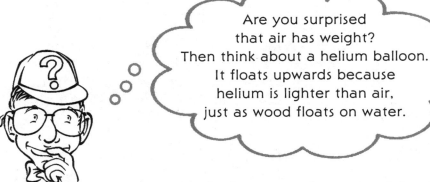

Are you surprised
that air has weight?
Then think about a helium balloon.
It floats upwards because
helium is lighter than air,
just as wood floats on water.

Meteorologists don't measure the total weight of the air around us, but rather the way that weight is spread out — or distributed — above different places on the ground.

They call that distribution of weight *atmospheric pressure*. Atmospheric pressure (sometimes called air pressure or *barometric pressure*, because it is measured by a device called a barometer) tells how much weight is in the column of air extending upward from a certain area on the Earth's surface to the edge of outer space.

Just as people report air temperature in different units (°F or °C) for different reasons, people describe the weight of the air above a certain area in several ways. In the United States, a common unit for air pressure is pounds per square inch, or *psi*. We'll start with that unit because it is easy to understand, but we'll soon shift to other units that meteorologists prefer.

If you live at sea level, the air pressure is typically 14.7 psi. From day to day and hour to hour, the pressure varies, but usually by only a little bit. It's almost never more than a few tenths of a psi from 14.7.

To understand how large that pressure is, set this book on a table, and imagine a rectangular column of air the size and shape of a page that goes all the way up from the book to the top of the atmosphere. The air in that column weighs about as much as six average-sized people. You could say the barometric pressure at sea level is about six person-weights per page.

Meteorologists usually use different units to measure pressure. For scientific use, they may use a metric unit called a *bar*. More commonly, however, they use a unit one thousandth as large, a *millibar*, usually abbreviated *mb*. Normal atmospheric pressure at sea level is 1013 mb, and hourly changes in air pressure are rarely more than a few mb. (Dr. Shepherd and other meteorologists who do research prefer an even smaller unit of pressure, the *Pascal*. One hundred Pascals equal one millibar.)

Weather forecasters usually report the barometric pressure in a different unit altogether — not psi, not millibars, not Pascals, and not person-weights per page. In the United States, you might hear something like this on the radio: "The barometric pressure, corrected to sea level, is 29.67 inches and falling." In Canada and other countries that use metric measurements, you might hear a number in millimeters instead of inches (around 754 in this case).

The number of inches or millimeters is the height of a column of the liquid metal mercury that weighs as much as all the air above it at that place. A one-inch square, 29.92 inch high column of mercury weighs 14.7 pounds. You might say that the normal air pressure at sea level is 14.7 psi, but you could just as well call it 29.92 inches (or 760 millimeters) of mercury.

Meteorologists want their barometer readings "corrected to sea level," because the higher you go, the less air is above you. The air pressure is measureably lower on the roof of a skyscraper than in the basement. Suppose you used a barometer for predicting the weather for that skyscraper. If you sometimes used barometer readings from the 72nd floor and sometimes from the lobby, you would end up with a bad forecast. You want your barometric measurement to tell you about changing weather conditions, not the changing distance of the barometer above the ground. To make it easy to interpret barometric readings from anywhere in the world, weather stations always report what the barometer would read if it were at sea level.

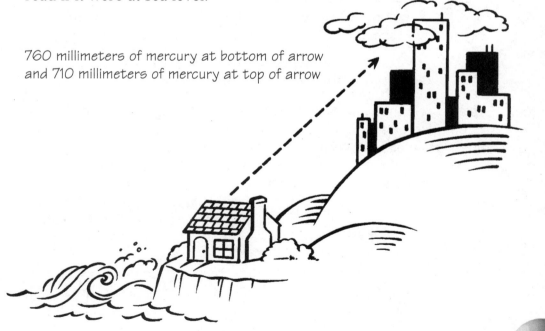

760 millimeters of mercury at bottom of arrow and 710 millimeters of mercury at top of arrow

Types of Barometers

The first barometer was invented by an Italian scientist named Evangelista Toricelli in 1643. He filled a long tube with mercury, then turned it upside down into a pan full of mercury so that its open end was under the liquid metal. The mercury began to run out of the tube, but it didn't all run out. Instead, it stopped when the height of the column of liquid mercury had fallen to about 29 or 30 inches above the level of the liquid in the pan.

Toricelli understood that pressure of the air above the mercury in the pan was equal to the pressure from the weight of the mercury in the column. Soon he discovered that the height of the mercury column varied from time to time. His instrument measured changing air pressure by the changing height of the mercury column.

WHY MERCURY?

Mercury is an unusual substance. It is a metal, but it is not a solid at ordinary temperatures. It is the heaviest of all liquids, 13.6 times as heavy as water.

If Toricelli had measured air pressure with a column of water, he would have needed a tube about 34 feet or 10.3 meters long!

Because we now know that mercury is a dangerous poison, it is rarely used in barometers.

Even so, weather forecasters still report the air pressure in inches or millimeters of mercury. Most barometers now are of a type called "aneroid," meaning without liquid. An aneroid barometer has a flexible chamber that contains trapped gas. When the atmospheric pressure increases, the chamber flexes inward. When the atmospheric pressure decreases, the chamber flexes outward. As the chamber flexes, an indicator attached to it moves. The indicator points to a scale that shows the pressure.

Once you calibrate the barometer for your altitude (distance above or below sea level), it always gives you the barometric pressure, corrected to sea level.

How to Make a Barometer

For your home weather station, you'll need a barometer. You could go to the store and buy one, but it's much more fun to make one for yourself. Here's how.

MATERIALS

- [ ] Scissors
- [ ] Medium-large uninflated balloon
- [ ] Mason jar
- [ ] Rubber band
- [ ] 8½ inch x 11 inch piece of cardboard
- [ ] Marker
- [ ] Super glue
- [ ] Drinking straw
- [ ] Shoe box
- [ ] Tape
- [ ] Ruler

To measure air pressure, we will construct a very simple but effective barometer. The most important measurement for predicting the weather is how fast the air pressure is rising or falling, and this barometer will measure that quite well. Therefore, it will be very useful for your weather station.

You will also be able to compare the readings of your barometer to the ones you hear on local weather reports. After a while, you will be able to use its readings as a measure of the actual barometric pressure, corrected to sea level.

STEP 1 Cut a slit from the mouth of the balloon to the end, so that you have a flat piece of rubber.

STEP 2 Stretch the balloon tightly over the mouth of the Mason jar, so the surface of the balloon appears flat. There should be enough of the balloon surface around the rim of the jar so that the rubber band can be used to seal it. A TIGHT SEAL IS VERY IMPORTANT.

STEP 3 Apply glue to the center of the stretched balloon and place one end of the straw firmly on the dab. Apply pressure until the glue is dry. The straw should point horizontally over the edge of the jar.

STEP 4 Tape the piece of cardboard to the face of the shoebox so that the cardboard stands on end. Move the cardboard so that it is next to the jar and aligned so that the straw runs along it.

With the marker, mark a dash at the point by the tip of the straw. Label that dash with the letter **R** for "reference" air pressure. All other pressures will be measured in comparison to it.

Next, mark a series of dashes one centimeter apart, both above and below the reference mark. Five on each side should be enough. From the reference mark upward, label each mark, **1H**, **2H**, etc. From the reference mark downward, label each mark **1L**, **2L**, etc. **H** stands for higher pressure and **L** for lower pressure. Finally, mark a series of dashes half-way between the labeled dashes.

This is what the finished experiment looks like.

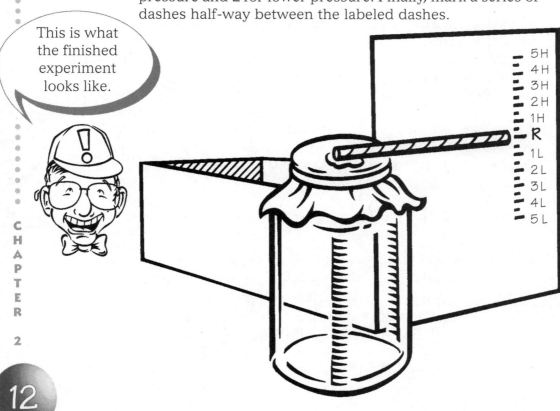

5H
4H
3H
2H
1H
R
1L
2L
3L
4L
5L

Reading Your Barometer

The barometer works because the air inside the jar is permanently trapped. If the outside pressure increases, it pushes the balloon skin downward. That tilts the straw upward. If the outside pressure decreases below the reference pressure, the air in the jar pushes the balloon skin outward, and the straw tilts downward.

Because the straw is longer than the jar is wide, it behaves like a lever, magnifying the short distance the balloon skin moves to produce a larger, more easily measured movement at the end. Surprisingly, this simple barometer responds to the range of air pressure changes typical of pressure systems and fronts.

As you use the barometer, you will be able to translate the markings from letters to actual values of the barometric pressure corrected to sea level. Pay attention to local weather reports from television, radio, or the internet. Note the reported air pressure and compare it to the barometer reading.

If the air pressure is steady or changing slowly, and your barometer is not too far from the official weather station, you will find that you have almost exactly the same pressure value every time your barometer points to a particular mark.

Changing marks into numbers is called *calibrating* your barometer.

That calibration will work well only when the barometer is used where the temperature is about the same all the time, such as inside a heated or air-conditioned home or building. You'll have a chance to discover the reason for that in the next chapter.

Experimenting With Your Barometer

DAILY UPS AND DOWNS

Since air pressure is the most important measurement for forecasting the weather, you should begin by using your barometer to notice how the pressure changes under different conditions. The first thing to do is to become familiar with the way the air pressure changes during the course of a typical day. Every hour, or at another convenient time interval over two or three days, observe and record the nearest mark to the end of your barometer pointer. The unlabeled in-between marks should be recorded as $\frac{1}{2}$ L, $1\frac{1}{2}$ L, $2\frac{1}{2}$L, etc., or $\frac{1}{2}$H, $1\frac{1}{2}$, $2\frac{1}{2}$, etc. Don't worry if you miss some measurements while you sleep.

Put these readings on a graph. The vertical axis should be labeled exactly the same way as the pressure scale on the barometer. The horizontal axis should be the time and date, each space to the right representing the passage of one more hour. After 24 spaces, you will reach the same time of day at which you started, but one day later. Draw a dark vertical line there to separate one 24-hour period from the next.

Although the actual pressure may change from one day to the next, you can observe that each day has a similar up-and-down pressure variation pattern (called a *diurnal pressure wave*).

The time that a day's highest and lowest pressures occur are usually the same day after day.

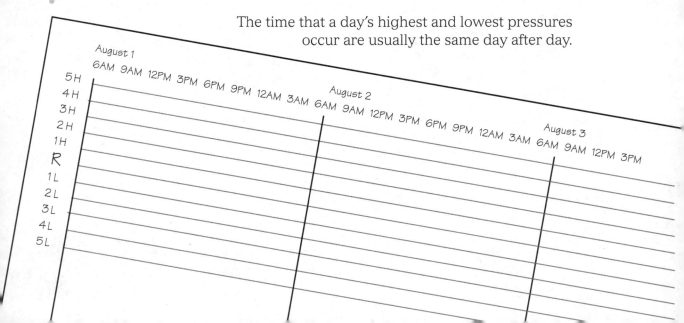

DETECTING A STORM

If the weather forecast is for a storm approaching, you can observe and measure the more rapid pressure changes that occur at that time. From three hours before the storm is due to reach you, observe and record the air pressure every fifteen minutes. From then until an hour after the storm reaches you, take measurements every five minutes.

Graph the results with each space on the horizontal axis standing for five minutes. The fifteen minute intervals will be three spaces apart. You will need about 48 horizontal spaces from the time you start measuring until the time you stop. You will see a different pattern of change in the barometer's response, much sharper than the diurnal pressure wave.

An airplane's *altimeter* — the gauge that shows how high the plane is flying — is a special kind of barometer.

MEASURING THE HEIGHT
OF A BUILDING OR A HILL

The higher you go, the less air is above you. Thus air pressure decreases when you go up to the top of a hill or a high building. Use your barometer to detect those changes. If you have calibrated your barometer and if the change in height is about 50 meters (about 165 feet) or more, you can make a reasonably accurate measurement. Measure the barometric pressure at the top and the bottom, then subtract the barometer reading at the top from the barometer reading at the bottom.

If your measurements are in millimeters of mercury, multiply that difference by 10.88 and round off to the nearest 10 meters to get the approximate height of the hill or building. If your measurement is in inches of mercury, the difference will be a small fraction of an inch. Multiply that number by 907 and round off to the nearest 25 feet.

These multipliers come from this simple fact: liquid mercury, a very heavy liquid, weighs 10,880 times as much as the same volume of air.

Air Pressure and Weather Forecasting

As you noticed in your
storm-detection experiment,
air pressure can be very useful
for understanding the weather.

An abrupt change in barometric
pressure is usually the signal
of a coming change in
atmospheric conditions,
also known as a "front."

Later in this book,
you will learn more
about the reasons for this.

For now, it's enough to say
that differences in air pressure
drive the winds and influence
the formation and development
of clouds, which may produce
rain or snow.

AIR PRESSURE FACTS,
FIGURES, AND PHENOMENA

Although air pressure is not as obvious in your life as temperature and humidity, your body does respond to changes in air pressure. Have you heard of or experienced any of the following?

▶ You may get a "sinus headache" — a pain in the spaces in the bones above and behind your nose — when air pressure changes.

▶ Your ears may "POP" when they experience rapid changes in air pressure, as when you ride in an airplane at takeoff or landing, in a car going up or down a long, steep hill, or in a high-speed elevator moving between floors in a tall building.

▶ Gases in your stomach may expand and need to escape when you go upward quickly and the air pressure around you drops. Dr. Fred says that drinking carbonated beverages in an airplane about to take off, a car about to climb a hill, or an elevator going up in a tall building might be a bad idea! (Burp!)

▶ An infected tooth can be painful when air pressure changes. Dr. Fred doesn't skip dessert, but he knows that this is a good reason to use a toothbrush after a sweet treat.

▶ Some people claim that sore muscles and joints are sensitive to air pressure changes. People with arthritis sometimes say they can feel a storm approaching in their bones.

Hurricanes are very large storms that develop over the oceans. As you probably discovered when you observed an approaching storm, the barometric pressure in a storm is lower than in fair weather air. Hurricanes are classfied according to the barometric pressure in their center or "eye." The classifications range from "minimal," in which the pressure is 735 millimeters (28.94 inches) of mercury or more, to "catastrophic," in which the barometric pressure is less than 690 millimeters (27.17 inches) of mercury. To experience a pressure that far below normal, you would have to go to the roof of a building about one and one-half times as tall as the World Trade Center in New York City.

Tornadoes are intense low pressure areas. They are much smaller than hurricanes, but their pressure changes much more sharply. Their winds can be up to 500 kilometers per hour (more than 300 miles per hour).

A "bomb" is a large storm or low pressure system in which the air pressure drops steadily for an entire day, not just the hour or two that you probably observed in your storm detection experiment. Bombs are typically found in the east coast area of the United States and in the western Pacific. Major snowstorms in the eastern United States are often caused by bombs.

During rainfall, raindrops evaporate and cool the air. Cooler air is heavier than warm air, so the rain causes a small rise in air pressure and high winds. You might feel this cool breeze, called a "gust front," just prior to rainfall.

The lowest barometric pressure ever recorded on a land station was 669 millimeters (26.35 inches) of mercury in 1935 during a hurricane. Lower pressures are probably found in the center of other hurricanes and tornadoes, but these are difficult to measure.

The highest pressure was 806 millimeters (31.75 inches) of mercury in 1893 at Irkkutsk, Siberia.

CHAPTER 3
TEMPERATURE

When most people get up in the morning and get ready to go out for the day, the first thing they think about is what to wear. Should they dress for cold, cool, comfortable, warm, or hot weather? What is the temperature now, they want to know, and what will it be later in the day?

To a scientist, heat and temperature have very specific meanings, but cold does not. Heat is a form of energy, and temperature measures how much heat energy is concentrated in one place. The more concentrated the heat energy, the higher the temperature. Scientists use the word cold in the same way you do in everyday conversation. It simply means that the temperature is low.

Heat energy can flow from one region in space to another. Like a ball rolling downhill, heat will naturally flow from a region of higher temperature to a region of lower temperature. It takes a machine and outside energy, like an electric refrigerator, to make it flow the other way. When two objects of different temperature come in contact, heat flows from the warmer one to the cooler one until they reach the same temperature.

Meteorologists like to use the term *gradient* to describe how sharply something is changing. The temperature gradient across a boundary is the difference in temperature divided by the thickness of that boundary. Not surprisingly, heat flows fastest when the gradient is sharpest — when the temperature difference is large and the boundary is narrow.

If you want to find dramatic weather conditions, look for places with sharp gradients in temperature and barometric pressure. In those places, you will find powerful movements of both air and heat.

Thermometers

A thermometer is a device to measure temperature. It includes at least one substance that changes in a predictable way when its temperature changes.

The most familiar thermometers use liquids like mercury or colored alcohol in a narrow glass tube. The tube has a bulb at the end that is filled with the liquid. Like the Glorpian metal of Chapter 1, the liquids take up more or less space — or volume — when the temperature rises and falls.

Since the bulb holds a lot of liquid compared to the narrow tube, a small change in the volume of the liquid leads to a big change in how far it goes up the tube. The thermometer-maker might design a thermometer so the liquid rises or falls one millimeter (about a twenty-fifth of an inch) for each degree. That's a small amount, but easily seen and marked on the glass.

Another kind of thermometer uses a long strip of two metals side-by-side, coiled into a spiral. The metals are chosen because their rates of expansion or contraction when heated or cooled are quite different. The metal on the inner side of the spiral is a bit shorter than the metal on the outer side, just as the road is longer around the outside of a curve than the inside. When the temperature rises or falls, the metals expand or contract at different rates. That forces the spiral to become more or less tight. An indicator attached to the spiral rotates and points to the temperature marks on a scale.

Old-fashioned home thermostats use "bi-metallic strips" to measure the temperature of the air. As temperature changes, the end of the strip bends to open or close an electrical switch, turning the heat or air-conditioning on or off as needed.

Digital thermometers are becoming quite common. Their temperature sensors are made of two strips of different metals, joined at one end but not at the other. That connection produces an effect like a battery whose electrical strength (voltage) changes as the temperature does. Its electronic circuitry transforms that voltage into a digital reading.

You can use any of these types of thermometers for your weather station. You may have a simple household thermometer available. Otherwise you can buy one in a hardware or home-improvement store. Make sure that the thermometer you select will be accurate and readable over the full range of outdoor temperatures for your region.

Buying a liquid thermometer has one significant advantage. In the chapter on humidity (moisture content of the air), you will have the choice of building two different kinds of instruments. One of them uses two identical liquid-bulb thermometers.

A digital thermometer has a different advantage. You can connect it directly to a home computer and record the results on a computer disk. Still, Dr. Fred doesn't like the idea of using one for this project. Part of the adventure and fun of building your own weather station is running outside on cold or rainy days to record your results.

HEAT, TEMPERATURE, AND MATTER

When scientists talk about heat and temperature, they also talk about the matter that makes up the Universe. Without matter, heat and temperature have no meaning.

As you probably know, every substance is made up of tiny particles called atoms or molecules. Those tiny particles are in constant motion even if the body they are part of is standing still. This back and forth motion has a certain amount of energy. That form of energy is called *heat*. *Temperature* measures the average heat energy per particle.

How to Make a Thermometer Shelter

To get an accurate temperature reading, you need to put your thermometer in a place where it measures the temperature of the air. By following these directions, you can build a shelter to keep the thermometer out of direct sunlight. Since the thermometer is attached to the shelter, you must design the shelter itself not to get warm in sunlight.

The United States National Weather Service makes its weather shelters out of wood painted white. The white paint reflects all colors of sunlight, so it absorbs very little of the energy of sunlight. Because wood does not conduct heat well, the small amount of heat that the outside of the shelter does absorb never reaches the thermometer inside.

MATERIALS

☐ Small common thermometer with cardboard or paper backing (Its temperature range should match your local climate.)
☐ White shoe box, without lid
☐ Glue or epoxy
☐ Typing or other plain white paper
☐ Tape

You could make a wooden shelter and buy a fancy thermometer, but a white cardboard shoe box and simple thermometer work almost as well. Dr. Fred's friend Marshall Shepherd became an expert weather-watcher with an inexpensive, simple thermometer and shelter, and so can you. You can follow these directions exactly, or you may modify them to accommodate a different kind of thermometer.

STEP 1 If the outside of the shoe box is not white, cover its bottom and sides with white paper, taped or glued into place. A good, reflecting white surface will keep the inside of the box from getting too hot, even in direct sunlight.

STEP 2 Place the shoe box on the floor or a table so the open end is up.

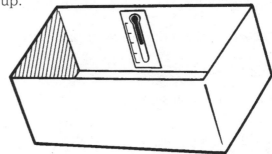

STEP 3 Glue the small thermometer, upside-down, to the inside center of the long side of the shoe box as shown.

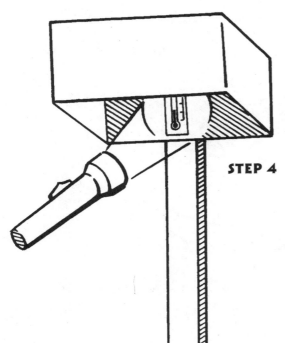

STEP 4 Turn the box over and attach it to a post several meters away from the house. The opening should be slighter farther off the ground than your eyes. Ideally, the box should not be in direct sunlight, and you should be able to read the thermometer easily. (You may need a small flashlight to illuminate it.)

EXPERIMENTING WITH TEMPERATURE

You may remember these words about calibrating your barometer in the last chapter: *"That calibration will work well only when the barometer is used where the temperature is about the same all the time."* Your first experiment with temperature is not with a thermometer, but with your Mason jar barometer. Here's the procedure:

STEP 1 While still indoors, put the Mason jar of the barometer in an empty pot that is about three-fourths as deep as the jar is high.

Note where the needle is pointing and record it.

Also note and record the temperature in the house or schoolroom according to the reading on the thermostat (the heating or air-conditioning temperature control) or an indoor thermometer.

STEP 2 Now surround the jar in the pot with ice from the freezer. Crushed ice, if available, will work better than ice cubes.

STEP 3 Watch the straw-indicator on the barometer change. The lower temperature will cause the pressure inside the jar to decrease, so the outside pressure should push the center of the balloon downward. That will make the indicator rise.

STEP 4 When the indicator stops rising, gently stir the ice or rotate the jar. The indicator may rise some more. When it finally reaches its highest point, note that reading. The temperature of the barometer is probably close to the freezing point of water (0°C or 32°F).

STEP 5 Subtract that freezing temperature from the temperature of the house or schoolroom. Count the number of lines that the indicator has risen. Finally, divide that into the temperature difference to get the number of degrees per line. For example, if the temperature in the house is 72°F and the indicator has risen from a reading of **1L** to a reading of **1 1/2H** — a total of 2 1/2 lines — then you get

$$\frac{72^{\circ}\text{F} - 32^{\circ}\text{F}}{2\,1/2 \text{ lines}} = \frac{40^{\circ}\text{F}}{2.5 \text{ lines}} = 16^{\circ}\text{F per line.}$$

STEP 6 Take the barometer outside. Set it on a well-shaded surface in the same empty pot you used indoors. Then allow its reading to settle down and make a note of that reading. Compare that reading to the original reading in the house or schoolroom. Use that reading to estimate the outside temperature.

Using the same example, let's suppose the barometer settles in at a reading of **1/2H**. That's 1 1/2 lines above the original temperature. At 16°F per line, that means it is 24°F colder outside, or about 48°F.

Compare that temperature with the temperature on your outside thermometer. How close are the two temperatures? Which one is likely to be more accurate? What have you learned about the calibration of your barometer?

DAILY AND SEASONAL CHANGES

Just as you began observing the daily pattern of air pressure changes with your barometer, you can do the same for temperature with a thermometer. Use the same notebook as you did with the barometer to record and preserve your observations. Every hour, or at another convenient time interval over two or three days, observe and record the temperature in your weather notebook. As before, don't worry if you miss some measurements while you sleep.

Put these readings on a graph similar to the one you used for the barometer. The vertical axis should be labeled to match the temperature scale on the thermometer. The horizontal axis should be the time and date, each space to the right representing the passage of one more hour. After 24 spaces, you will reach the same time of day at which you started, but one day later. Draw a dark vertical line there to separate one 24-hour period from the next. Although the actual temperature may change from one day to the next, you should be able to observe that each day has a similar up-and-down temperature variation unless a weather front passes through.

Since the sun's heat affects the temperature, be sure to note sunrise and sunset on the graph. Also mark the point halfway between sunrise and sunset as "solar noon" and the point halfway between sunset and the next sunrise as "solar midnight."

Note when the daily high and low temperatures occur in comparison to those four time markers. Over a period of several months, you will begin to see not only the daily ups and downs of temperature but also how the pattern of temperature variation changes from season to season.

COMPARING YOUR TEMPERATURE
TO THE "OFFICIAL" READING

When Dr. Fred's friend Marshall Shepherd learned to predict the weather for his little town of North Canton, Georgia, he discovered that the temperature was usually different from the official temperature at the National Weather Service station at the Atlanta airport. You will probably find that the same is true for your weather station.

On the same graph paper that you use to record the hourly temperatures at your home weather station, use a different colored pencil or ink to record the "official" temperature, which you may be able to find on the radio, television, or worldwide web. If you have a computer connection, the web is probably the best place, because you can find a record of the temperature and its changes at a more convenient time, hours or perhaps days after those measurements were made.

THINK LIKE A SCIENTIST!

Compare temperature graphs you have
made of the official temperature
and the temperature at your station.

Do you see a relationship between them?

Is the temperature at your weather station
usually higher or lower than the official reading?

When the temperature changes rapidly, does it happen
first at your home weather station or the official one?

Those questions will point out the differences in temperature
between your weather station and the official one.

Dr. Fred's challenge to you is this:
Develop a theory — an idea that can explain the differences.
Then think of ways to test whether that theory is right.

AIR PRESSURE FACTS, FIGURES, AND PHENOMENA

▶ The hottest temperature ever recorded on Earth was 136°F (58°C) at El Azizia, Libya on September 13, 1922.

▶ The hottest temperature ever recorded in the United States was 134°F (57°C) at Death Valley, California. This is also the hottest temperature ever recorded in the Earth's entire Western Hemisphere. Death Valley is the only place in the United States where nighttime temperatures remain above 100°F.

▶ The coldest temperature ever recorded on Earth was −129°F (−89°C) at Vostok, Antarctica on July 21, 1983.

▶ The coldest recorded temperature in the United States was −80°F (−62°C) at Prospect Creek, Alaska on January 23, 1971.

▶ On January 21, 1918, the temperature in Granville, North Dakota, went from −33°F (−36°C) to 50°F (10°C) in twelve hours.

▶ On January 19, 1892, the temperature in Fort Assiniboine, Montana, went from −5°F (−21°C) to 37°F (3°C) in fifteen minutes!

▶ In colder weather, jet airliners do not need as long a takeoff distance as when it is warm.

▶ The Earth's climate seems to be warming. The 1990s was the warmest decade in history and scientists are measuring melting of both polar ice caps.

MEASURE TEMPERATURE LIKE A SCIENTIST

Scientists prefer to measure temperature on the Celsius scale, but if you live in the United States, you will probably hear weather reports in Fahrenheit degrees. Your thermometer may also be marked in Fahrenheit. How can you convert temperature measurements from one scale to the other?

You begin by looking at two conditions where you know what the temperature readings should be. The freezing point of water is 0°C or 32°F. The boiling point of water is 100°C or 212°F. Between the two temperatures are 100 Celsius degrees or 180 Fahrenheit degrees. Thus for every increase of one degree Celsius, the temperature rises by 1.8 (or $9/5$) degrees Fahrenheit. Since the Fahrenheit reading is 32 more than Celsius at freezing, you can write this formula:

$$F = 1.8 \times C + 32 \text{ (or } 9/5 \times C + 32\text{)}$$

That gives you the Fahrenheit temperature if you know the Celsius temperature. To go in the opposite direction, you take the difference between the Fahrenheit temperature and freezing. Then divide that by 1.8 (or multiply by $5/9$) to get the difference between the Celsius temperature and freezing. Since freezing is 0°C, that difference is the Celsius temperature. Written as a formula, that means:

$$C = (F-32)/1.8 \text{ or } 5/9 \times (F-32)$$

Here are some other examples to try.

1. What is the Fahrenheit temperature that corresponds to 20°C?

2. What is the Celsius temperature that corresponds to the normal human body temperature of 98.6°F?

3. What is the Fahrenheit temperature that corresponds to -40°C?

Find the answers at the bottom of the next page.

Answers to questions on page 31

1. 68ºF   2. 37ºC   3. –40ºF

CHAPTER 4
AIR MOVEMENT

Wind is the motion of the air.
In the last chapter, you read about heat, which is the back-and-forth motion of molecules; but wind is motion of a different kind. It's the movement of a mass of air from one place to another. The molecules inside that mass still move back and forth in every direction, but the mass also moves as a whole from one place on Earth to another.

It is as if you and a friend are playing ping-pong on a moving cruise ship. The back-and-forth motion of the ball is like the heat — or thermal motion — of the molecules. The motion of the boat and everything it carries with it — including you, your friend, and the table you are playing on — is like the wind.

Barometric Pressure and Wind

In the last chapter, you read about temperature gradients — the sharpness of changes in temperature from one region to another — and you read that heat energy naturally flows from a higher temperature to a lower one.

Another important kind of gradient is a "pressure gradient." Pressure gradients drive the movement of air masses. Heavy winds are associated with strong or "steep" pressure gradients; light winds occur when pressure gradients are smaller. The wind is the movement of air masses away from high pressure areas toward low pressure areas.

Just as a ball rolling down a steep hill gains more speed than one rolling down a gentle one, wind flowing "down" a steep pressure gradient blows faster than when the pressure gradient is more gradual. The more air that flows, the more powerful is the wind it creates.

Think back to your experiment with the barometer when the storm front was passing through. You probably remember that the barometric pressure fell quickly as the air mass passed your weather station. That means the pressure gradient was steep, which is why the wind was strong as the front passed.

If you have ever released air from a bicycle tire, you have witnessed a pressure gradient creating wind. The air inside the bicycle tire is at a much greater pressure than the air outside the tire. When you depress the little stem inside the valve, the high pressure air inside rushes out towards the region of lower pressure air. The "rush" continues until the pressures are equalized and the tire is "flat." You can hear and feel the motion of the air, which is on a small scale the same thing that happens when the wind blows. In the case of the tire, the gradient is very steep — much steeper than ever occurs in the atmosphere, but the amount of air moving is small.

Local and Global Winds

If you want to predict the weather for your neighborhood, you need to understand not only the air movement in a small area, or the local wind, but also air movements all around the world. Winds are driven by pressure gradients. One kind of pressure gradient is known as a "front." Fronts are boundary lines in the air between regions with different weather conditions. They form when high and low pressure air masses move toward each other. As a front passes your neighborhood, you can expect strong local winds.

Geography also affects local winds. For instance, if you live near an ocean or a large lake, you probably know about the daily breezes that blow in from or out towards the water. In sunlight, land heats up faster than water. At night, land cools faster than water. The air above the land and water follows that same temperature pattern.

Since warm air is lighter than cool air, the air pressure is lower over the warmer region and higher over the cooler one. Breezes blow from the higher pressure region towards the lower one — from the cool to the warm. On a hot summer afternoon, the sea or lake breezes bring cool air inland. At night, after the land has cooled, the breeze goes back the other way.

Hills or mountains can also affect your local winds. By forcing the air to rise, they can also influence the way clouds form (Chapter 5). In cities, local winds can also be affected by tall buildings (the air has to go around and over them) or large paved areas (they absorb more heat from sunlight than ordinary ground). If you want to become a neighborhood weather expert, pay attention to any natural or human-made feature that can affect the way the wind blows and the way clouds form.

Global winds are driven by the energy from the sun and the rotation of the earth. As you probably know, the earth rotates, or spins around, once per day on its axis, an imaginary line passing through its north and south poles. It also travels in a huge, nearly circular path — or orbit — around the sun, completing that journey in a year. If you think of the orbit as a flat disk, the earth's axis doesn't point straight up and down. Instead, it is tilted.

That tilt causes the seasons. On the first day of summer in the northern half (or "hemisphere") of the world, the north pole is tilted as far towards the sun as it ever gets. On that same day, the south pole is tilted as far away as it gets, so it is the first day of winter in the southern hemisphere.

All season long, the summer half of the planet gets more sun than the winter half. On the first day of spring and fall, the tilt is neither toward the sun nor away from it. Rather the axis tilts along the edge of the orbit, so neither hemisphere gets more than the other.

Halfway between the poles, separating the northern and southern hemispheres, is the equator, an imaginary circle around the earth. Sunlight at the equator is always more direct than at the poles. The sun is most direct at the places on the earth when it is overhead at noon. Those places shift from north to south and back again as the seasons change. The regions where most direct sunlight can occur are called the tropics.

When the sun is overhead in a tropical region north or south of the equator, the opposite polar region (either between the north pole and the Arctic Circle or between the south pole and the Antarctic Circle) has days without sunlight. That darkness lasts from nearly two days to half a year, depending how far from the pole the place is.

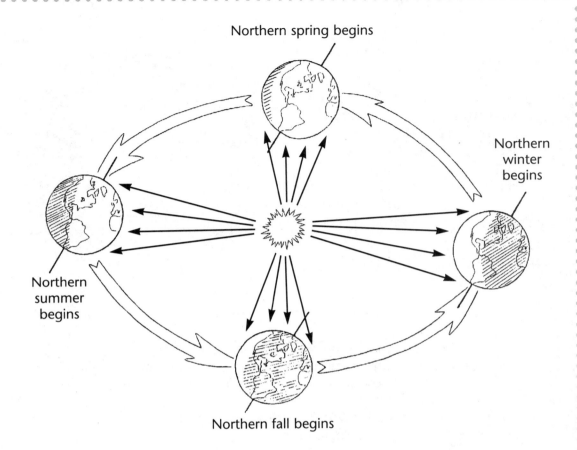

Northern spring begins

Northern winter begins

Northern summer begins

Northern fall begins

Between the tropics and the polar regions are the temperate zones, where the sun rises and sets every day but is never directly overhead. Since the heating patterns of these three regions of the earth — polar, temperate, and tropical — are very different, the air temperature varies. Cold air is heavier than warm air. That means the pressure at the poles tends to be higher than the pressure at the equator.

If the earth didn't spin, the pressure difference would move the air in a north-south direction from poles to the equator. Instead the earth's rotation causes a swirling pattern of the winds. As the diagram on the next page shows, surface winds move generally west-to-east in the temperate regions and east-to-west over the tropics and the poles.

The pattern of those "prevailing winds" shifts northward and southward with the changing seasons. Those winds move weather fronts from place to place. The prevailing wind patterns are important for predicting the movement of storms or fair weather systems.

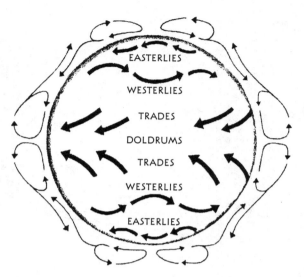

EASTERLIES
WESTERLIES
TRADES
DOLDRUMS
TRADES
WESTERLIES
EASTERLIES

When sailing ships crossed the oceans from east to west and back again, the crews depended on their knowledge of the prevailing winds. Getting caught in the doldrums, where the winds were very light, could spell trouble.

Air movement also can be up and down. These "updrafts" and "downdrafts" are important in the development of clouds and storms, and you will read more about them in later chapters.

How to Make a Wind Vane and Anemometer

**An adult should be present
when you make these instruments.**

Your weather station needs instruments to measure both the speed
and the direction of the wind. A wind vane shows the direction
that the wind is blowing, and an anemometer shows how fast it is
blowing. These will probably be the least reliable
of your instruments, but they will still provide
you with useful measurements for
forecasting the weather to come.

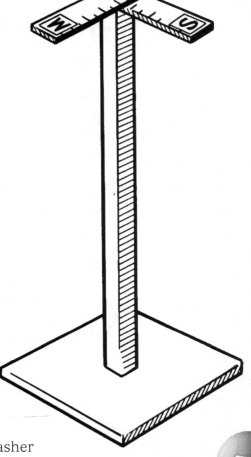

Wind Vane

MATERIALS

☐ 1 foot x 1 foot
   (30 centimeter x 30 centimeter) piece
   of wood ³/₄ inch (2 centimeter) thick

☐ 4 foot (125 centimeter) long piece
   of 2 inch x 2 inch (5 centimeter x
   5 centimeter) lumber

☐ 1 yardstick, meterstick, or
   similar sized piece of lumber

☐ 2 1 ¹/₂-inch (4 centimeter) nails

☐ 2-inch (5 centimeter) thin nail

☐ Hammer

☐ Sipping straw

☐ Piece of cardboard
   or back of a writing tablet

☐ Scissors

☐ Construction paper

☐ Marker

☐ Glue or epoxy

☐ ¹/₂-inch (1.25 centimeter) metal flat washer

MAKING THE STAND

STEP 1 Drive a 1 1/2-inch nail through the foot-square wood into the center of one end of the 2 x 2-inch lumber.

STEP 2 Set the foot-square piece on the ground with the 4-foot long piece standing vertically upright.

MAKING THE DIRECTION MARKER

STEP 1 Cut the yardstick into two equal halves.

STEP 2 Criss-cross the two halves, forming a horizontal plus sign resting on top of the stand. Align the edges of the yardstick with the edges of the stand, and place the center of the plus sign over the center of the stand.

STEP 3 Carefully drive the other 1 1/2-inch nail through the plus sign into the top of the vertical piece, a bit off center. This leaves room for the other nail, which will go through the center later.

STEP 4 Rotate the base so the two halves of the yardstick are aligned north-south and east-west

STEP 5 With the markers, draw squares containing the letters N, S, E, and W on the construction paper, making them just a bit narrower than the yardstick. These will designate the four directions: North, South, East, and West.

STEP 6 Cut and glue the letter squares to the appropriate ends of the yardstick.

MAKING AND MOUNTING THE POINTER

STEP 1 Gently hammer the thin 2-inch nail a short distance (about $1/4$ inch or $1/2$ centimeter) into the center of the plus sign, so the majority of it is sticking up.

STEP 2 Slip the metal washer over the nail.

STEP 3 Use the marker to draw an arrow shape on the cardboard, about 6 inches (15 centimeters) long and 2 inches (5 centimeters) wide. Cut out the arrow. This will be mounted vertically as the pointer.

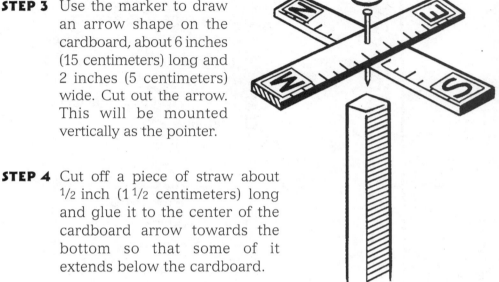

STEP 4 Cut off a piece of straw about $1/2$ inch ($1\,1/2$ centimeters) long and glue it to the center of the cardboard arrow towards the bottom so that some of it extends below the cardboard.

STEP 5 Slip the straw over the nail so the arrow is mounted and is free to rotate in the wind. It will point in the direction the air is moving. Assuming the wind is blowing in the same direction at your weather station as at the official one, the arrow will point to the opposite direction of the weather report. If the winds are from the west, the air is moving towards the east, so the arrow points to E.

(You could, of course, turn your base around so the direction markers indicate the opposite of the actual direction. Then when the wind is from the west, the arrow will point to the letter **W** at the eastern end of the direction marker.)

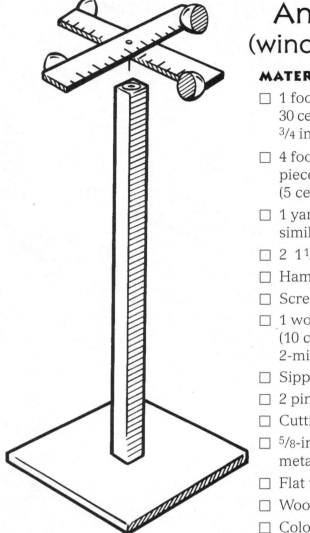

Anemometer
(wind speed meter)

MATERIALS

☐ 1 foot x 1 foot (30 centimeter x 30 centimeter) piece of wood 3/4 inch (2 centimeters) thick

☐ 4 foot (125 centimeter) long piece of 2 inch x 2 inch (5 centimeter x 5 centimeter) lumber

☐ 1 yardstick, meterstick, or similarly-sized piece of lumber

☐ 2 1 1/2-inch (4-centimeter) nails

☐ Hammer

☐ Screwdriver

☐ 1 wood screw, 4 inches (10 centimeters) long with 2-millimeter threads

☐ Sipping straw

☐ 2 ping-pong balls

☐ Cutting utensil

☐ 5/8-inch (1 1/2-centimeter) metal flat washer

☐ Flat thumbtacks

☐ Wood glue

☐ Colored paint

MAKING THE STAND

STEP 1 Drive a 1 1/2-inch nail through the foot-square wood into the center of one end of the 2 x 2-inch lumber.

STEP 2 Set the foot-square piece on the ground with the 4-foot long piece standing vertically upright.

MAKING THE SPINNER MOUNTING

STEP 1 Make a hole in the center of the top of the stand about 2 inches (5 centimeters) deep and wide enough to hold the straw.

To do that, repeatedly screw and remove the wood screw until you have made a hole large enough for a drinking straw to fit and about 2 inches (5 centimeters) deep.

STEP 2 Cut 2 inches (5 centimeters) from a drinking straw, and insert that piece in the hole.

STEP 3 Glue the metal washer to the top of the wood piece such that the washer surrounds the hole with the drinking straw.

MAKING THE SPINNER

STEP 1 Cut the yardstick into two equal halves.

STEP 2 Criss-cross the two halves, forming a plus sign.

STEP 3 Carefully drive a $1\frac{1}{2}$-inch nail through the center of the plus sign all the way through both portions. For ease and safety, you may want to temporarily remove the straw from the hole and set the plus sign over the hole, letting the nail poke all the way through. The nail will be the axis on which the spinner will turn, but the spinner is not yet complete.

STEP 4 If you removed the straw to drive the nail, remove the incomplete spinner from the hole and reinsert the straw.

STEP 5 Insert the incomplete spinner into the spinner mounting. It should rest on the washer and spin easily when pushed.

STEP 6 Cut the two ping-pong balls in half. These half-balls will catch the wind when attached to the spinner arms.

STEP 7 Tack each half-ball through its center to the end of an arm of the spinner as shown. The tack should go into the side of the yardstick, and the open face of the half-ball should be exposed. Start by tacking one half-ball, then rotate the spinner through a quarter-turn, tacking the next half-ball in the same place and direction as the previous one. Repeat until all four half-balls are in place.

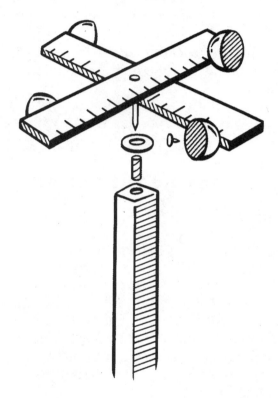

STEP 8 Apply glue to secure the half-balls onto the arms of the spinner. After the glue dries, blow gently into one of the half-balls to make sure the spinner turns easily in the wind.

STEP 9 Paint one of the half-balls so you will be able to keep track of which is which. You are now ready to measure wind speed.

MEASURING THE WIND
WITH YOUR WIND VANE AND ANEMOMETER

As noted, these instruments will probably be the least accurate of all the parts of your weather station. The anemometer also requires some practice and calibration before you can get good wind-speed measurements from it.

Have you ever walked down a street in the downtown section of a major city and felt a powerful blast of wind as it flows between skyscrapers? Those buildings channel the air movement, affecting both the wind speed and direction, like rows of big rocks might do to the flowing water of a stream. Homes and buildings in your neighborhood may have similar but much smaller effects.

A nearby row of trees can also make accurate wind measurement difficult. Therefore, you'll need to place your wind vane and anemometer in a convenient place as far as possible from homes, buildings, and other human-made structures. If you live in a city or the suburbs, an open space in a backyard or school playground will probably be the best you can manage.

Another problem with measuring wind is the anemometer itself. Friction, the rubbing force between the parts of a spinning anemometer, may affect its speed. Also, the measurement is best made when the wind is steady, which is not always the case.

Nevertheless, it is possible to measure wind speed and direction well enough to draw some useful conclusions about the weather to come. Measuring wind direction is not difficult. You simply note the direction the vane is pointing. If it is not pointing directly along one of the four main directions, it's easy to estimate northeast, southeast, northwest, or southwest.

Measuring wind speed with the anemometer is much more difficult, and it takes practice. You begin by counting how many revolutions (full turns) per minute (abbreviated rpm) the anemometer makes. You could try to count the revolutions while watching the second hand of a watch go around once, but you're likely to lose count or to be uncertain about whether to count all or part of the last revolution. A better technique is to choose a point to start, say when the colored half-ball passes in front of you. Glance at the watch, and note where the second hand is. Then count revolutions up to ten, twenty, thirty, or some other convenient number.

When that number of revolutions has been completed, note the position of the second hand and compute the number of seconds from start to finish. Then multiply the number of revolutions by sixty. Finally divide that result by the number of seconds. That gives the anemometer's rpm. Since you are likely to be off by a second or so in your timing, round off the rpm to the nearest whole number.

For example,

if thirty revolutions take 47 seconds, you multiply $30 \times 60 = 1800$.

Then divide 1800 by 47 and get 38.297872 if you use a calculator.

All those numbers after the decimal point don't mean a thing, so you call the result 38 rpm.

Wind Speed and the Beaufort Scale

After you feel confident in your rpm measurements, you can begin to calibrate the anemometer. To do that, you start with a wind-speed scale first developed in 1805 by a British Admiral named Francis Beaufort. As the table on page 49 shows, Beaufort developed a scale ranging from 0 (calm) to 12 (hurricane) based on the way common objects responded to the wind. Over nearly two centuries since, scientists have been able to use better and better equipment to measure wind speed and to attach miles-per-hour or kilometers-per-hour numbers to Beaufort's scale.

To calibrate your anemometer, observe the wind whenever you can over several days or weeks. You probably will be able to go outside safely with your wind gauges when Beaufort scale readings range from 0 through 5. On the rare occasions when the Beaufort reading goes to 6 or beyond, it will probably be too stormy for your equipment. Just use the Beaufort scale instead.

When measuring the wind, first note the Beaufort scale reading by watching how things move in the wind. Then measure the rpm of your anemometer. Repeat the measurement several times and record both rpm and Beaufort readings in your weather logbook. Keep a page or part of a page for each Beaufort scale reading, listing the measurements of anemometer rpm for that reading. After a while, you will find that each Beaufort number corresponds to a particular range of rpm.

Because your Beaufort measurements will not be precise, your rpm ranges for each Beaufort number will overlap a little bit with the numbers above and below. But eventually, you will be able to develop a reasonably good relationship between anemometer rpm and miles or kilometers per hour. That is your calibration.

AIR MOVEMENT FACTS, FIGURES, AND PHENOMENA

► Alaska is the windiest state in the United States; more of its weather stations are on the list of places with the highest average wind speeds than any other state.

► The highest wind ever recorded at the Earth's surface was 231 miles (372 kilometers) per hour atop Mt. Washington, New Hampshire, 6262 feet (1909 meters) above sea level. Average wind speed there is 35 miles (56 kilometers) per hour.

CALIBRATION USING THE BEAUFORT SCALE

Beaufort #	Km per hr	Miles per hr	Description	Observation	Anemometer rpm range
					(You fill in this column based on your data)
0	0 – 1	0 – 1	Calm	Smoke rises straight up	
1	1 – 5	1 – 3	Light Air	Smoke drifts; leaves barely move	
2	6 – 11	4 – 7	Slight breeze	Leaves rustle; wind felt on face	
3	12 – 19	8 – 12	Gentle breeze	Leaves and twigs move; paper bits and dust rise	
4	20 – 28	13 – 18	Moderate breeze	Small branches move	
5	29 – 38	19 – 24	Fresh breeze	Small trees sway; dust clouds rise	
6	39 – 49	25 – 31	Strong breeze	Large branches sway; hard to use umbrellas	*(Don't try taking data from here on)*
7	50 – 61	32 – 38	Moderate gale	Whole trees sway; hard to walk	
8	62 – 74	39 – 46	Fresh gale	Twigs break off trees	
9	75 – 88	47 – 54	Strong gale	Tree branches break; slight damage to buildings	
10	89 – 102	55 – 63	Whole gale	Trees blown down; buildings heavily damaged	
11	103 – 117	64 – 72	Storm	Widespread damage	
12	118 – up	73 – up	Hurricane	Extreme damage	

CHAPTER 5
MOISTURE IN THE AIR

So far, your home-made weather station has instruments to measure the wind and the pressure and temperature of the air. Now it's time to pay attention to water. We'll start by measuring precipitation: water that falls in the form of rain, snow, sleet, or hail. Later, we'll look at how to measure the water that doesn't fall but stays in the air as vapor.

Rain, sleet, snow, or shine?

When you get ready to go out for the day, what's the first thing you want to know about the weather? Will it be sunny or cloudy, clear or stormy. How much rain or snow will we get?

Snowfall is usually easy to measure because it piles up and stays where it falls. You can measure its depth with a ruler or meterstick. Snow depth can be tricky, because the amount of water in it can vary. It can be packed and heavy or fluffy and light. Meteorologists usually measure not only the snow depth, but also the amount of water in it by melting it. The water in snow is about as much as in one tenth as much rain. For example, ten inches of snow has about as much water as an inch of rain.

How to Make and Use a Rain Gauge

If you live in a typical North American city, the total rainfall in your area is about 40 inches (100 centimeters) per year. That's an average of about an eighth of an inch or about 3 millimeters per day. Although some days may produce more than an inch of rain, many days are just drizzly. If you put out a pot to collect a day's worth of rain or snow, the water in it would be too shallow to measure accurately. It would be just about impossible to tell whether one day's drizzle amounted to more than another's.

For your weather station, you need to be able to do better than that. The trick is to collect rain or snow over a wide area and put it into a narrow container, where it will be much deeper. You can make a simple, accurate rain gauge using a ruler, a kitchen funnel, and two glass jars of different sizes.

MATERIALS

☐ Empty Mason jar or a jar of similar size and shape
☐ Kitchen funnel
☐ Empty olive jar or another straight, tall, narrow jar
☐ Ruler
☐ Calculator or pencil and paper

CALIBRATE THE INSTRUMENT

STEP 1 Use the ruler to measure the diameter of the funnel (across the inner rim of its wide opening). You can use inches, but the arithmetic will probably be easier if you use millimeters.

STEP 2 Use the same ruler and the same units of length to measure the diameter of the olive jar across the inside of its opening.

STEP 3 Divide the diameter of the funnel by the diameter of the olive jar. That gives a number called the diameter ratio.

STEP 4 Multiply the diameter ratio by itself. That result is the ratio of the area of the funnel to the area of the olive jar. Record that number to the nearest tenth and call it the calibration ratio.

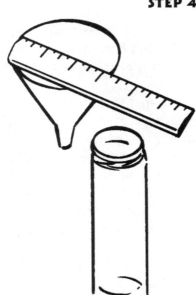

Diameter ratio = 18/8 = 2.25

Area ratio = 2.25 x 2.25 = 5.0625

Round off 5.0625 to get calibration ratio = 5.1

COLLECT THE RAIN

STEP 1  On a rainy day, place the kitchen funnel inside the Mason jar and set it outside where it will collect rainfall. Choose an open space as far from trees or buildings as possible to catch all the rain, but to avoid catching drips. Note the time you start collecting and the time you stop.

STEP 2 Transfer the rain water from the Mason jar to the olive jar using the funnel.

STEP 3 Using the ruler, measure the depth of the water in the olive jar in inches or millimeters.

STEP 4 Divide that depth by the calibration ratio. Record that result to the nearest hundredth of an inch or tenth of a millimeter. That is the measured rainfall.

How much water is in 1 centimeter of rain?

Have you ever wondered how much water falls on your yard in a rainstorm? Here's a calculation that may be surprising. The arithmetic is much easier in metric units, but you can convert to inches and pounds at the end.

Mark a 1-meter square in your yard, just to see how large a square meter is. Imagine that square meter is covered by 1 centimeter of water, the amount that might fall on a typical rainy day. Since 1 meter is 100 centimeters, the square has an area of 100 x 100 or 10,000 square centimeters. 1 centimeter of water on that area would have a volume of 10,000 cubic centimeters or 10 liters. Since 1 liter of water weighs 1 kilogram, that square meter would be covered with 10 kilograms of water.

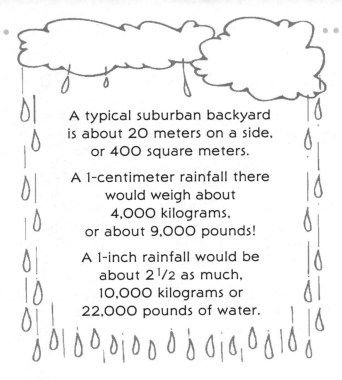

A typical suburban backyard is about 20 meters on a side, or 400 square meters.

A 1-centimeter rainfall there would weigh about 4,000 kilograms, or about 9,000 pounds!

A 1-inch rainfall would be about 2 1/2 as much, 10,000 kilograms or 22,000 pounds of water.

EXPERIMENTING WITH YOUR RAIN GAUGE

How long should you sprinkle?

You can use your rain gauge to measure the time that you should use your lawn sprinkler in one spot. In many areas of North America, people need to water their lawns in the summertime to keep the grass green. Suppose your lawn needs about a 1/2 centimeter (nearly 1/4 inch) of water every day. You can use your rain gauge to measure the amount of water your sprinkler is delivering.

Put the rain gauge in the middle of the sprinkler pattern and collect water for 15 minutes. How much "rainfall" did it create in that time? Use that result to compute how long you should run the sprinkler before moving it to the next area.

Moist Air, Dry Air, and the Dew Point

Rain and snow are water in its liquid and solid forms, but water also can exist as a gas. At high temperatures, it can boil and become steam; but at lower temperatures it can also exist as a vapor — a gas that mixes with the other gases in the air.

The best way to understand water vapor is to think about a puddle of water on a warm sidewalk after a rain. Right before your eyes, the puddle begins to shrink as the water evaporates. How does that happen?

Like all molecules in any substance, the molecules of water in the puddle move back and forth. Every once in a while, a molecule moves fast enough to escape the surface and go into the air. That's evaporation, and the evaporated water is called *water vapor*.

THE CASE OF THE DISAPPEARING SNOW

You've seen puddles dry up, and you know that is due to evaporation. You may have also seen snow disappear when it is too cold to turn into a puddle first. Just as fast water molecules escape from an evaporating puddle into the air, the same thing happens — but more slowly because there are fewer fast molecules — to ice and snow. That transformation from solid water to water vapor is called *sublimation*.

Humidity is a measurement of how much water vapor is in the air. The air can hold only a certain amount of water vapor. The warmer it gets, the more water vapor it can hold. Most commonly, you will hear about *relative humidity*, which is the amount of water vapor in the air as a percentage of the total amount it can hold. You feel sticky when the air temperature and relative humidity are both high. Your body perspires from the heat, but the perspiration can't evaporate easily because the air can't hold much more water vapor.

When the air holds all the water vapor it can, it is said to be saturated and the relative humidity is 100 percent. If the temperature of saturated air drops, it can no longer hold as much water. Some of the water then condenses back into a liquid or a solid.

You can see condensation form on the outside of a cold beverage glass and on the bathroom mirror after you take a hot shower, or you can see it as the morning dew or as frost.

We use the term "dew point" for the temperature to which we would have to chill the air for dew or frost to form. The higher the relative humidity, the closer is the dew point to the air temperature.

Measuring Humidity

The best way to measure relative humidity is to measure and compare the air temperature and the dew point. A device that measures relative humidity is called a *hygrometer*. A particularly accurate kind of hygrometer has two identical thermometers on a handle that allows you to spin them rapidly. Around the bulb of one thermometer is an absorbent cloth that you moisten with water before spinning. Just as your evaporating perspiration cools your skin, the evaporating water cools the wet-bulb thermometer down to the dew point.

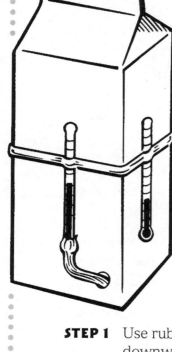

Making a Simple Hygrometer

You can make a simpler version of that hygrometer. Instead of spinning it to evaporate the water on the wet bulb, you will fan it dry.

MATERIALS

- ☐ 2 identical household thermometers that use colored alcohol as the indicator fluid
- ☐ Empty cardboard milk or juice carton
- ☐ A shoelace
- ☐ Rubber bands
- ☐ Water
- ☐ A small piece of stiff cardboard

STEP 1 Use rubber bands to attach the thermometers, with their bulbs downward, to two sides of the carton next to each other.

STEP 2 Cut a section of the shoelace about 6 inches (15 centimeters) long and slip it over the bulb of one of the thermometers. That will be the wick of the wet-bulb thermometer.

STEP 3 Cut a small hole near the bottom of the side of the carton where the wet-bulb thermometer is attached.

STEP 4 Push the bottom of the wick through the hole so that it rests on the bottom of the carton.

STEP 5 Pour enough water into the carton so the wick is covered. Allow a few minutes for it to draw enough water through it to wet the bulb.

STEP 6 Use the stiff cardboard to fan the wet bulb for at least 5 minutes. Quickly read the temperature of both thermometers. Use the graph on the next page to determine the relative humidity.

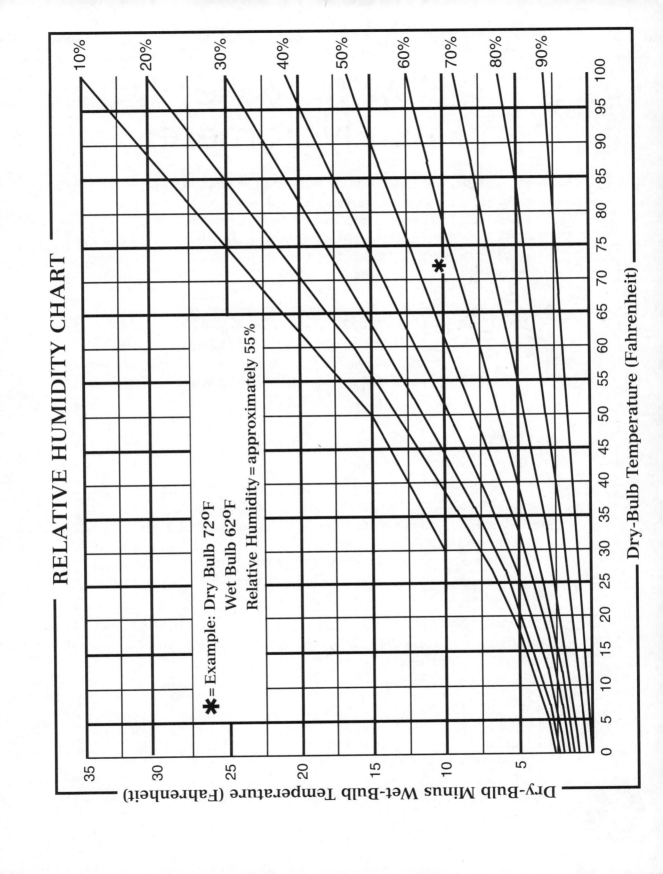

RELATIVE HUMIDITY CHART

✱ = Example: Dry Bulb 72°F
Wet Bulb 62°F
Relative Humidity = approximately 55%

Dry-Bulb Minus Wet-Bulb Temperature (Fahrenheit)

Dry-Bulb Temperature (Fahrenheit)

10%
20%
30%
40%
50%
60%
70%
80%
90%

How to Make
a Hair Hygrometer

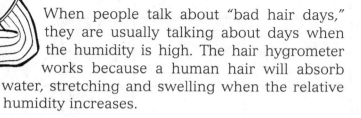

When Marshall Shepherd built his weather station, he made a different kind of hygrometer, one that depends on the behavior of a human hair. It is more complex and requires calibration, but it is probably more accurate than the milk carton hygrometer. It is definitely more fun to build and calibrate.

When people talk about "bad hair days," they are usually talking about days when the humidity is high. The hair hygrometer works because a human hair will absorb water, stretching and swelling when the relative humidity increases.

MATERIALS

- ☐ 1 quart, dry cardboard milk carton
- ☐ 2 small buttons
- ☐ 3-inch long (7.5-centimeter) darning needle
- ☐ Small makeup mirror, approximately 3/4 inch (2 centimeters) in diameter (Don't try to remove a mirror that is part of a "compact." A mirror designed to fit in the base of a lipstick tube would be ideal.)
- ☐ Popsicle stick or tongue depressor
- ☐ Sipping straw
- ☐ Superglue
- ☐ A human hair, at least 10 inches (25 centimeters) long, natural blond is best
- ☐ Small straightened paper clip
- ☐ Masking tape
- ☐ Graph paper
- ☐ Ruler
- ☐ Warm soapy water

PREPARE THE HAIR AND THE CARTON

STEP 1 Wash the hair in warm, soapy water, then rinse it. This is necessary to strip the hair of any oils or chemicals.

STEP 2 Open the top of the milk carton, rinse it, and allow it to dry. Then tape the top in place so it is flat.

STEP 3 Lay the milk carton on one side as shown with its original bottom towards the right.

STEP 4 Cut three long, rectangular openings for ventilation in the top and two sides of the carton, as shown.

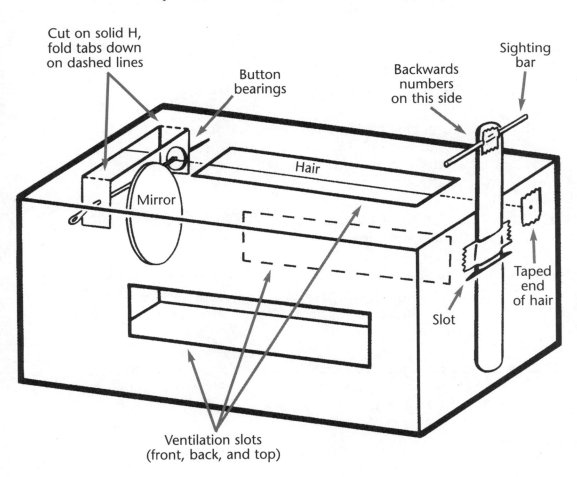

Cut on solid H, fold tabs down on dashed lines

Button bearings

Backwards numbers on this side

Sighting bar

Hair

Mirror

Slot

Taped end of hair

Ventilation slots (front, back, and top)

MAKE THE AXLE BEARING

STEP 1 In the left portion of the side of the carton that is now on top, cut a small H (as shown in the drawing on page 61), 5 centimeters (2 inches) long by 2.5 centimeters (1 inch) wide. This creates two square tabs that can be bent downward as shown, opening a slot.

STEP 2 Glue a small button to each tab as shown. The buttons will form an axle bearing with the needle as the axle.

STEP 3 Pass the needle through the buttons. Make sure the needle can turn freely and easily by rotating it until the holes in the cardboard are smooth and loosened.

ATTACH THE MIRROR AND THE HAIR

STEP 1 With the help of an adult, glue the back of the mirror to the center of the needle. The glue should be near the top of the back of the mirror so that it will hang vertically under its own weight (refer to the illustration on page 61).

STEP 2 Using a drop of glue, attach one end of the hair to the needle near the mirror. Allow the glue to dry.

STEP 3 After the glue dries, turn the needle two or three complete turns, winding the hair around it. The front surface of the mirror should be facing the original bottom of the carton when this is done.

STEP 4 Make a hole in the original bottom of the carton and thread the other end of the hair through. Make it taut, and tape it to the milk carton.

MAKE THE MEASUREMENT SCALE

STEP 1 Glue a strip of graph paper to a popsicle stick. Hold the stick so that the scale will be vertical, and number the lines on the graph paper 0 to 20 from top to bottom. *You will be viewing the numbers in the mirror, so write them backwards.*

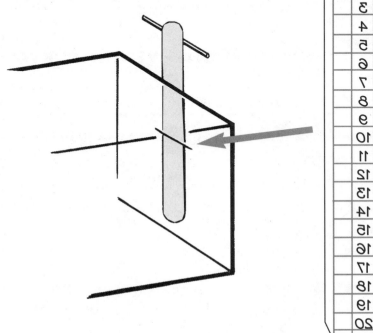

STEP 2 Cut a slit, into which you will insert the scale, in the upper portion of the right end of the carton. The large numbers should be near the bottom of the carton and zero should be near the top.

STEP 3 Tape the scale in position with masking tape. At the top of the scale, tape the straightened paper clip horizontally. This will form a sighting gauge.

STEP 4 Adjust the mirror by removing the taped end of hair, and pulling on it until the number 10 is on the line of sight. Then retape the hair in place.

> This procedure will set three points on the humidity scale. Get all three set points on the same day when it is not raining or snowing.

CALIBRATION — VERY IMPORTANT!

PART I Setting the 100% point

STEP 1 Take the hygrometer to the bathroom and close the door.

STEP 2 Run the shower with hot water for fifteen minutes to be certain the air reaches 100% relative humidity.

STEP 3 Read the value from the sighting gauge. That value represents 100% relative humidity.

PART II Determining a humidity point in the middle of the scale using the local weather service value for your area

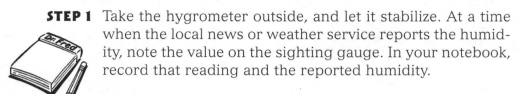

STEP 1 Take the hygrometer outside, and let it stabilize. At a time when the local news or weather service reports the humidity, note the value on the sighting gauge. In your notebook, record that reading and the reported humidity.

PART III Setting a low humidity point

STEP 1 Place the hygrometer in the freezer for two minutes. Remove it, and quickly take a reading. This scale value corresponds to 10%.

PART IV   Creating a measurement chart

STEP 1 On a piece of graph paper, make a graph with relative humidity (0 to 100%) on the vertical axis and the hygrometer scale readings from 0 to 20 on the horizontal axis.

STEP 2 Put three dots on the graph, one for each of the three calibration points from PARTS I, II, and III

STEP 3 Connect the points with two straight lines to make a measurement chart, like the one shown here.

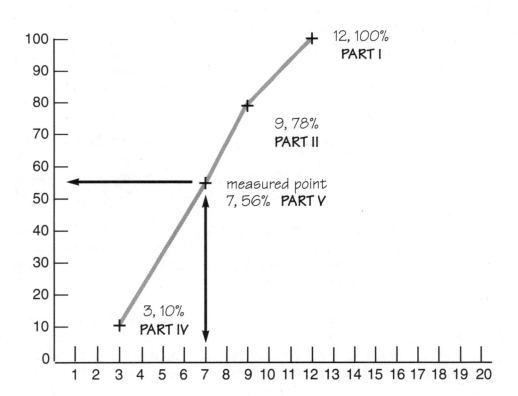

STEP 1   When you take a humidity measurement, use the chart as follows.

STEP 2   Find the hygrometer reading on the horizontal axis.

STEP 3   Draw a vertical line upward from that value to the point where it meets the line on the chart.

STEP 4   Draw a horizontal line from that point leftward to the vertical axis

STEP 5   The value on the vertical axis where that horizontal line meets it corresponds to the relative humidity.

In the example shown on page 65, the calibration points are (3, 10%), (9, 78%), (12, 100%) and the humidity reading is 7. Using the chart, that corresponds to a humidity of about 56%.

EXPERIMENTING WITH HUMIDITY GAUGES

Here are two exercises to familiarize you with your hygrometer, no matter which of the two you choose to build.

Monitor the humidity values approximately hourly (except when you are sleeping) with your hygrometer for a 24-hour period. Determine if there are any trends or noticeable rises and falls. Can you explain the changes?

At the same time you are monitoring your hygrometer, record the temperature, pressure, and humidity as reported by your local radio, television, or weather service. Does your hygrometer seem to be accurate? Do humidity variations seem to be related to changes in temperature or pressure? If so, describe the relationships.

PRECIPITATION AND HUMIDITY
FACTS, FIGURES, AND PHENOMENA

▶ Three stations in the United States with highest annual average precipitation

Yakutat, Alaska — 135 inches (343 centimeters)

Hilo, Hawaii — 128 inches (320 centimeters)

Annette, Alaska — 115.5 inches (293 centimeters)

▶ Three stations in the United States with lowest annual average precipitation

Yuma, Arizona — 2.65 inches (6.73 centimeters)

Las Vegas, Nevada — 4.19 inches (10.64 centimeters)

Barrow, Alaska — 4.75 inches (12.07 centimeters)

▶ World's highest annual average precipitation

Lioro, Columbia — 523.6 inches (43 feet, 7.6 inches or 1329 centimeters)

▶ World's lowest annual average precipitation

Arica, Chile — 0.03 inch (0.075 centimeter),

or about as much in a year as Lioro gets in an average half-hour!

▶ World's largest "cloudbursts"

Most rain in a minute, 1.5 inches (3.8 centimeters) — Nov. 1970, Barot, Guadeloupe, West Indies

Fastest foot of rain, 42 minutes — June 22, 1947, Holt, Missouri

Most rain in 10 hours, 140 centimeters (55.1 inches) — Aug. 1, 1977, Muduocaidang, Nei Mongol, China

▶ Longest "dry spell" in the United States — 767 days from October 1912 to November 1914 in Bagdad, Arizona

► Longest "dry spell" in the world — more than fourteen years from 1903 to 1918 in Arica, Chile

► Snowiest places in the United States, outside of Alaska, annual averages:

Blue Canyon, California — 240.8 inches (611.6 centimeters)
Marquette, Michigan — 126.0 inches (320.0 centimeters)
Sault St. Marie, Michigan — 116.4 inches (295.7 centimeters)

► Central Florida has the most annual days with thunderstorms in the United States

► Floods kill more people each year than hurricanes, tornadoes, wind, or lightning

► If you could squeeze all the water out of a cubic yard of saturated air at 95°F, you would collect only an eighth of a cup of liquid

CHAPTER 6
FORECASTING THE WEATHER

Now that you've built your weather station, you are ready to become a weather watcher.

Watching and measuring the weather is the first step in making weather forecasts.

Keeping a Weather Log

As you became familiar with your instruments, you probably also got used to keeping records in your weather log book. Now it's time to put everything together in a way that you can use it.

Until you begin keeping detailed records, you will not understand the weather in your area as well as you think you do. No matter where you live, weather conditions change rapidly and vary widely from day to day and season to season. Where Dr. Fred lives, it never snows from late May until late September, and the temperature normally is below freezing on a mid-winter day. Still, he sometimes needs a warm coat on a rainy, chilly day in July, and he can sometimes take a walk without a jacket in January. Those unusual days are the ones he remembers best. That's probably true for you, too.

Since your memory will emphasize unusual days, you need to keep written records to discover what is normal for your neighborhood. A weather log will have measurements of both normal and unusual conditions. Neighborhood weather experts never rely on memory alone; they depend on written records. Nothing is more valuable than a well-kept log.

You can begin your official neighborhood weather record with the chart on the facing page. It can be copied and used daily. It has space for you to keep track of barometric pressure, temperature, relative humidity (and the dew point if you use a wet-bulb thermometer), wind speed, wind direction, precipitation, and cloud conditions. The earlier chapters have prepared you to measure all of those, except for the clouds. On pages 78–83, you can read about different kinds of clouds and the kinds of weather they indicate.

Daily Weather Watcher Chart

Date _____

Date	Time	Barometric Pressure (sea level)	Air Temperature	Dew Point Temperature	Wind Speed	Wind Direction	Cloud Cover or Type	Current Weather Condition and Comments

Notes:

As you gain experience, you may decide to develop a different format. If you are skilled with computers, you may decide to keep records on your hard drive or on diskettes. You might even create a computerized data base of your neighborhood weather, from which you can easily find past conditions or develop statistics. The more you know about your neighborhood weather history, the better you will do predicting the weather to come.

It also will help if you know how your neighborhood weather compares to the weather at nearby official weather stations. Thus you will want to include official readings in your weather log as well as your own weather readings. After a while, you'll discover whether your neighborhood is usually warmer or cooler than the official station and by how much.

When changes in the weather come, you will discover whether your neighborhood sees the change before or after the official station, and you'll learn how long it takes the change to move from one place to the other.

The Earth's Atmosphere, Climate, Weather Systems

After you understand how your neighborhood's weather fits with a nearby weather station, the next step is to learn how it fits with weather in the rest of the world.

Weather maps show large masses of air that move together, which meteorologists call *weather systems*. These are areas of high or low barometric pressure, usually labeled H and L. High pressure areas usually mean fair weather. Low pressure usually means clouds and storms.

Because the Earth spins, the air in these systems swirls. In the northern half of the Earth, air usually flows clockwise and downward in high pressure systems and counterclockwise and upward in low pressure systems. In the southern half, the direction of the swirling is opposite, but the upward or downward motion is the same.

As the air in a Low rises, it cools. The cooler it gets, the less moisture air can hold. Thus if the air in a Low is humid, it soon cools to the point that it can no longer hold water vapor. Clouds of tiny waterdroplets or ice crystals form, floating on the rising air. These clouds grow, and, eventually, the droplets or crystals become too large to stay in the air. They fall to Earth as rain, sleet, or snow.

In Highs, the air warms as it falls. Any waterdroplets or ice crystals that it might be carrying become clear water vapor, and the weather is fair.

Colliding Air Masses = Stormy Weather

To understand what happens when two air masses meet, you need to know a little bit about air density, which means the weight of a particular volume of air. Air, like all gases, expands as it warms. That means the same weight of air occupies more space, or the same space contains less weight than before. Warm air is lighter (or less dense) than cold air.

It may surprise you that humid air is lighter than dry air at the same temperature. That is because the weight of a molecule of water is much less than the weight of a molecule of nitrogen or oxygen, the gases that make up most of the air. The more water molecules in the mixture, the lighter is its average weight. For that reason, humid air is associated with low pressure areas and dry air is associated with high pressure areas.

When two air masses collide, the result is an unstable boundary region between them. Meteorologists call that region a *front*, because it is the leading edge of a change in the weather. If a mass of warm air overtakes colder air, the lighter warm air rides over the cold air, creating a warm front. As the warm air goes higher, it begins to cool, so it can no longer hold as much moisture. That leads to clouds and sometimes light precipitation. The more warm air that advances, the lower and thicker the clouds become, and the precipitation may be heavier. Then, after the warm front passes, warmer, drier air follows. A barometer would indicate a high pressure area has arrived.

A cold front usually produces more dramatic weather. The heavier cold air shoves the warm air rapidly upward, and the warm air's moisture quickly condenses into clouds and heavy precipitation. If the cold air mass is large and fast moving, this may cause severe storms and rapidly falling barometric pressure.

Detecting Weather Systems
and Making Forecasts
with Your Weather Station

Since weather fronts bring quick changes in barometric pressure, the barometer is the most useful instrument for detecting their approach and passage. If you did the experiments with your barometer in Chapter 2, you probably noticed how fast barometric pressure changed when a rainstorm approached and passed your weather station.

Now that you have a full weather station, it's time to pay attention to the entire set of changes when a front goes by. When the weather forecast on your local radio or television station warns that a front is approaching, begin to make frequent measurements with all your instruments. In your log book, describe the changing cloud pattern and record barometric pressure, temperature, humidity, wind speed, and wind direction. These will probably change rapidly, so keep detailed and careful records.

Over several weeks, you will be able to observe the passage of several fronts. Soon you will begin to recognize a pattern of changes that accompanies a warm front and a different pattern that accompanies a cold front. By studying those patterns, you will be able to use your weather station measurements to identify the kind of weather front that is approaching. You will be able to anticipate precipitation and changes in temperature or other weather conditions. Your weather watching will have begun to produce useful forecasts for your neighborhood.

Using Weather Maps and Other Data

Your weather station may be useful for predicting the weather a few hours in advance, but you can't make a longer-range forecast without information on weather in the rest of the world. Weather systems travel across entire continents and oceans, bringing changes that can be predicted days in advance.

To make a detailed forecast, you need detailed information about atmospheric conditions around the world. Today, thousands of weather watchers in different places around the planet report conditions — some with basic instruments and others with very sophisticated ones.

Modern technology is very important in weather prediction. Weather satellites measure the atmosphere in many ways. They take photographs of dangerous storms from space, giving people warning in time to evacuate threatened areas.

Sophisticated radar systems spot severe thunderstorms and tornadoes as they are forming. Meteorologists then warn people in the danger zone to find shelter. People have written programs for supercomputers that produce forecasts with greater accuracy every year.

The amount of weather information is amazing. Even more amazing for young weather watchers is that they can get most of the same information as professional forecasters. Satellite images and weather station measurements from around the world are now available to anyone with a computer connection to the Internet and the world wide web.

When Marshall Shepherd was a schoolboy forecasting the weather for North Canton, Georgia, he had to rely on weather maps for his long range forecasting. His information was very limited. If he was doing that science fair project today, his problem would be the opposite. He would be able to get far more information than he could handle. How could he select the information to use and where on the web would he go to get it?

Those questions are the subject of this book's last chapter, and no one is better equipped to answer them than Marshall Shepherd himself. His love of the weather took him from North Canton Elementary School to the Georgia State Science Fair to a career as a meteorologist with NASA. Now some of his observation instruments are orbiting the Earth. He hopes someday to take his weather-watching instruments to new heights and fly with them on the International Space Station.

So read on and discover Dr. Shepherd's thoughts on how you can become an expert weather watcher. Who knows how far it might take you!

All About Clouds

Cloud-watching is one of a weather forecaster's most interesting and enjoyable tasks. By watching those masses of tiny water-droplets and ice crystals move and change, you can begin to understand the flow of moisture and air at many levels. If you live near a large body of water or a mountainous area, cloud-watching can even show you how local terrain influences the weather.

Clouds form when air cools down to the dew point. That usually happens in an updraft when two weather systems meet. At high levels in the atmosphere, above 15,000 feet (about 5 kilometers) or so, the air is thin and the wind speed is high. Clouds that form there spread out quickly, usually forming long shapes that may be feathery or curly in appearance. These are called *cirrus* clouds after the Latin word for curly.

When more water vapor collects in unstable air, clouds begin to grow upwards and take on a lumpy or puffy appearance. Those clouds are called *cumulus,* because of the accumulation of water in them.

A third type of cloud formation is spread out into layers. These are called *stratus,* which means stretched or spread out. Clouds below 6,500 feet (2 kilometers) are usually of this type and have a high water content.

Meteorologists begin their classification of clouds with those three terms, but go beyond that. They use the term "alto-" from the Latin word for high to describe clouds in the middle range 6,500–26,000 feet (2–8 kilometers). For dark, storm clouds, they use the term *nimbus,* Latin for "rain cloud." The following pages show the cloud types described in the table on page 83.

HIGH CLOUDS

Cirrus

Cirrostratus

Cirrocumulus

MIDDLE CLOUDS

Altostratus

Altocumulus

LOW CLOUDS

Stratus

Stratocumulus

Nimbostratus

TALL CLOUDS

Cumulus

Cumulonimbus

Cloud type	Description	Type of Weather to Expect
Cirrus	Long, thin, feathery, high	Fair
Cirrostratus	High, gauze-like; ring may form around Sun or Moon	Fair
Cirrocumulus	Groups of puffy cirrus (resembles fish scales; called "mackerel sky")	Storm may follow
Altostratus	A broad, thick, layer that almost hides the sun	Warm front with rain in several hours
Altocumulus	Puffy clouds with distinct edges; form groups resembling waves	Watch for nimbostratus to come; morning altocumulus may mean afternoon thunderstorms
Stratus	Low, gray, may cover the sky	Watch these change into other forms
Stratocumulus	Low, broad sheets, lumpy blobs	Clearing (stratus or cumulus breaking up)
Nimbostratus	Stratus with darker, rougher base	Front is arriving; light to moderate precipitation for several hours
Cumulus	Puffy, often with flat bottom marking height at which air temperature is at the dew point	Light, brief showers
Cumulonimbus	Very tall, towering (up to 40,000 feet or 13 kilometers in height), dark base, may have flat icy top that fans out downwind	Heavy storm, violent weather, hail, high winds, lightning and thunder likely. Very dangerous weather possible

CHAPTER 7

FROM WEATHER WATCHER TO METEOROLOGIST

If you would stop reading now, you would have a simple weather station, a good log book, and a guide to clouds. All you would need to qualify as a neighborhood weather watching expert is to take measurements and keep records for a year or two. You would be able to listen to the forecast for a nearby city and decide how the forecast might differ for the street where you live.

But young weather watchers usually don't stop with that. If you are like Marshall Shepherd was at your age, you'll already be looking for more information. You'll dream of better instruments and computer connections. You'll look forward to the day when you, like Dr. Shepherd, can proudly carry the title of Meteorologist.

Dr. Fred asked Dr. Shepherd to imagine that he was back in school doing this project. Where would he go for more information? How would he improve his equipment? How would he begin the journey from neighborhood weather watching to meteorological research?

The rest of this chapter is based on what Dr. Shepherd wrote in response to those questions. Because the locations of information on the world wide web can change quickly, Dr. Fred will provide updates to this information, as well as other useful information about books and science, in the "Books by Dr. Fred" section of his own world wide web site

http://www.FredBortz.com

Advice from Dr. Shepherd
Direct to You

It is fun and educational for you as young "weather watchers" to make measurements of the weather in your neighborhood. You can use your home-made weather watching instruments to learn about the current neighborhood weather conditions (temperature, humidity, pressure, and wind) and how these conditions relate to past, current, and future weather.

Unfortunately, weather conditions are constantly changing in time and in location. Weather watchers 50 miles (or less) in different directions from your neighborhood may find very different weather conditions from you and from each other.

Weather systems that create the daily weather are constantly developing, changing, or dying. This makes forecasting the weather in your neighborhood a difficult job. Meteorologists use many additional resources to understand the current and changing weather in and around their towns, cities, and states.

The exciting news is that many of these resources are available to your "neighborhood weather watch" as well. You can connect personal computers in your libraries, schools, and homes to the Internet and world wide web.

You can get Doppler radar imagery from the National Weather Service and weather satellite imagery from NOAA (the National Oceanic and Atmospheric Administration) and NASA (the National Aeronautics and Space Administration). You can find weather maps, weather data, and computer software.

In this chapter, we will explore some of the neat Internet and computer resources available to you as part of a worldwide weather watch network. We will help you discover exciting interactive and "hands-on" weather sites that will help make you the most accurate weather forecaster in your neighborhood.

Finally, we will share useful information that will help you to go from "amateur" weather watcher to weather hobbyist. From there, you may even go on to become a forecaster, TV weathercaster, or a meteorological research scientist.

Weather Watching Beyond Your Neighborhood

The weather instruments you have built can provide you with a picture of the current conditions in your neighborhood. However, if you want to make accurate forecasts of what will happen next, you need to see what's going on beyond your own backyard.

Suppose there is a cold front 100 miles to the west of your neighborhood causing strong rain and thunderstorms. If you have good information about its speed and direction of movement, you will be able to predict if and when it will affect you. You might get that information from Doppler radar imagery, satellite imagery, and weather maps showing the areas surrounding your town, city, or neighborhood.

Doppler radar is a large microwave transmitter and receiver that sends out pulses of microwave energy into clouds. Some of that energy bounces off the rain or snow and reflects back to the radar.

The receiver creates a colorful display with lots of useful information from the reflected pulses.

Ordinary radar just detects where the reflecting objects are. Doppler radar also detects how fast they are moving toward or away from the detector. For a distance of a few hundred miles in each direction, it shows where precipitation is falling and where strong winds or rotation (like tornadoes) are present.

When several radar images are combined, you can figure out how fast and in which direction storms are moving. To learn more about Doppler radar, you can visit sites such as the USA Today Weather Topics Index at

http://www.usatoday.com/weather/windex.htm

and search for "Doppler radar."

Weather satellites orbit the Earth taking pictures of cloud systems in both visible and infrared light. Visible light cameras see the cloud systems in the same way that your eye sees this page. Infrared cameras "see" the clouds, even at night, by measuring the temperature of the cloud tops. Colder cloud tops are usually associated with rainfall. From space, we are able to see what is happening in a very large area of the world.

Most commonly, weather satellites are launched into "geostationary" orbits at a height of about 22,400 miles (about 36,000 kilometers) above the planet. At that height, it takes them exactly one day to complete their orbit, so they remain above the same latitude at all times. Since they can view an area thousands of miles across at one time, they can constantly monitor clouds over the entire United States mainland. (In different geostationary orbits, other satellites watch weather over Europe and much of Africa. Still others orbit over other parts of the world.)

For more information on weather satellites plus links to interesting satellite images, visit

http://rsd.gsfc.nasa.gov/goesb/chesters/web/goesproject.html/

At many other sites on the world wide web, you can find real-time radar and satellite imagery to help you forecast weather changes in your neighborhod by seeing the weather that is heading your way. You may have to explore those sites a bit to find the data, but exploring them can be both educational and fun. Some of the best sites include the following:

The Weather Channel	http://weather.com
CNN Interactive	http://cnn.com
The WeatherPost	http://www.weatherpost.com
EarthWatch	http://www.earthwatch.com
WeatherNet	http://cirrus.sprl.umich.edu/wxnet
Intellicast	http://www.intellicast.com/weather/usa

Weather maps are another useful tool for showing weather conditions over large areas. The National Weather Service (NWS) collects weather data at cities around the country using instruments similar to but more accurate than the ones you made.

The most useful maps are those showing pressure systems. The maps have lines on them, called *isobars*, that connect points with the same barometric pressure. Fronts show up as places where the isobars are close together. Maps with lines of constant temperature (isotherms) are also valuable, although local terrain may affect temperature in certain places.

The best on-line locations to find and study surface weather maps are:

WeatherNet	**http://cirrus.sprl.umich.edu/wxnet**
USA Today	**http://www.usatoday.com/weather**
The Weather Channel	**http://weather.com**
CNN Interactive	**http://cnn.com**
National Weather Service	**http://www.nws.noaa.gov**
Weather Underground	**http://www.wunderground.com**

An enjoyable and educational exercise for young weather watchers is to create local weather maps for your area. This requires you to find weather watchers in several neighborhoods separated by a few miles.

You would probably need ten or more weather stations to be able to create a useful map. Perhaps several schools in one area could work together, exchanging information by e-mail.

- Begin by drawing or finding a map of your area and mark the location of each weather watch station.

- Make several copies of that map, which you will use to create surface weather maps. Keep one copy for reference or for making more copies later.

- Agree on a schedule for taking measurements. All weather watchers will take measurements in their separate locations at the same time. For a few days, log the temperature, pressure, humidity, wind, and rainfall amount, then compare your results.

- Draw isobars on one map, isotherms on another, and lines of constant relative humidity on a third. On a fourth, draw arrows showing wind direction with the length of the arrow representing the wind speed. If a weather front was passing through the area at the time, it should show up on all the maps in different ways. Can you see it?

Beyond Surface Maps. Weather patterns at the surface usually depend on conditions at higher levels of the atmosphere. Meteorologists also measure wind, pressure, temperature, and moisture patterns at different altitudes. For those, they use radiosondes, special balloons that carry instruments that measure the standard weather variables (pressure, temperature, humidity, wind speed, and direction) and send the information back to the ground by radio signals.

This data from sites around the country can be used to create maps similar to surface maps for different levels of the atmosphere. This allows meteorologists to study the effects of upper air phenomena, like the high altitude wind called the *jet stream,* on the surface weather. You can learn about the Jet Stream in the Weather Basics section of the *USA Today* on-line weather information pages,

http://www.usatoday.com/weather.

Good sites for finding and studying upper air maps include:

WeatherNet   **http://cirrus.sprl.umich.edu/wxnet**

WeatherWorld   **http://members.aol.com/Accustiver/wxworld.html**

Other NWS Information. All neighborhood weather watchers should keep in touch with their local NWS office. These offices issue weather measurements, special weather statements, and other information that are intended specifically for their local area.

Your skill as a neighborhood forecaster will depend on knowing how your measurements compare to those official local measurements. You can visit your area's NWS on-line service through the following sites:

NOAA/NWS Sites   http://www.nws.noaa.gov

Interactive Weather   http://iwin.nws.noaa.gov/iwin/iwdspg1.html

Many of the sites mentioned throughout this chapter, but specifically the National Weather Service and WeatherNet sites, also include a variety of forecast maps and data generated by the weather service's large weather prediction computer models. How do those computer programs use real measurements to produce daily, weekly, and monthly forecasts? You can visit NOAA's environmental site (http://www.noaa.gov/env1.htm) to find out.

Other Useful Web Resources for the Weather Watcher

Any good weather forecaster takes advantage of as many available resources and as much real data as possible. This section provides a listing of additional on-line resources that you may find useful to your weather observation and forecasting projects.

http://www.weatherpost.com/longterm/reference.htm

The *Washington Post* Weather Reference is an excellent reference site. It contains a weather glossary with over 600 terms and a valuable definitions/explanation page. It also provides a weather calculator to perform simple but essential calculations like: Fahrenheit-Celsius Conversion, Wind Speed Conversion, Heat Index (a measure of the discomfort level on hot, humid days), and Wind Chill (a measure of how cold the air would feel to your uncovered skin when the wind blows).

http://www.usatoday.com/weather

The *USA Today* on-line weather information pages have clear weather explanations and diagrams, plus a weather glossary and weather library.

http://vortex.plymouth.edu/clouds.html

The Plymouth (New Hampshire) State College meteorology program site has a good set of cloud pictures to help the weather watcher understand and identify clouds. It also discusses what types of weather may be associated with different types of clouds. This is a highly recommended site for the amateur weather watcher.

http://ww2010.atmos.uiuc.edu/(Gh)/guides/mtr/home.rxml

The University of Illinois meteorology guide is a very good site for tips on weather forecasting. It provides general forecasting methods and information on how to read weather maps. It also provides good education modules to understand weather and climate systems.

http://members.aol.com/Accustiver/wxworld_forecast.html

This "Weather World" page is another excellent source of step-by-step guidelines for weather forecasting.

http://www.weatherpost.com/historical/historical.htm

The *Washington Post* weather history site provides historical weather data for over 2,000 cities worldwide. Information included in the database are statistics on temperature, rainfall, snow, humidity, and other variables.

http://athena.wednet.edu/curric/weather/index.html

The Athena Earth and Space Science K-12 education program's weather page allows students to observe, track, chart, and forecast weather systems interactively. Try it!

http://www.nssl.noaa.gov

The National Severe Storms Center site is probably the most complete site for information on observing, tracking, and forecasting severe weather (such as thunderstorms, lightning, and tornadoes). If you ever wondered what "storm chasers" were looking for besides thrills, this site has the answers.

http://www.nhc.noaa.gov/index.html

The National Hurricane Center site is one of the best places to learn about hurricanes and how they are observed, tracked, and forecast. There is a wealth of educational material and downloadable hurricane tracking charts. If you are the type of weather watcher who loves to track hurricanes, be sure to blow into this site during the season.

http://members.aol.com/Accustiver/wxcam.htm

Weather World has links to live views from over 800 weather cameras around North America. If you want to see what weather is occurring in a neighborhood or town other than your own, this is the place to visit.

http://sln.fi.edu/weather/activity.html

Philadelphia's famed Franklin Institute Science Museum has weather activities and experiments that you can try at home. It also has a very comprehensive listing of all types of weather links. (http://sln.fi.edu/tfi/hotlists/weather.html)

http://www.ncdc.noaa.gov/extremes.html

If you liked the Facts, Figures, and Phenomena sections in this book, you will enjoy exploring the weather extremes pages of the National Climatic Data Center. It also has information about air and ocean conditions that influence the Earth's climate in important ways, such as the notorious "El Niño."

How to Upgrade your Neighborhood Weather Watch

After getting your neighborhood weather watch "up and running," and after exploring some of those sites on the web, you are probably boiling with excitement. You may even be ready to become a full-fledged "weather weenie," someone who is so crazy about the weather that the simple weather station you built here is no longer enough.

If you are ready to spend some time and money to upgrade your neighborhood weather watch, here's some information about more advanced weather stations, weather software, and the professional contacts in the field of meteorology.

Weather Stations. Commercially available weather stations range in price from a few dollars to thousands of dollars. The low-priced items will not be very different from the one you built here, and they'll be less fun; but you don't have to spend a fortune to upgrade your weather station.

If you decide to invest in better weather equipment, first check with your parents about how much they are willing to spend. Then shop carefully, and don't buy anything without your parents' approval.

The first step is to show them what you have already done and explain to them why you are ready for better equipment. If you do that right, you may discover that at least one parent is a weather weenie just like you.

Weather stations are also available at many hobby stores, museums, and gift shops. Before you go to a store, you might want to look at the following sites on the worldwide web to see what is available.

We aren't endorsing any of these sites, but visiting them will help you understand what weather instruments and software are available in a variety of price ranges to expand or build your weather observatory.

http://www.weathermarket.com/index.htm
Weather Information Systems, Amity, OR

http://www.columbiaweather.com/WeatherStations.html
Columbia Weather Systems, Hillsboro, OR

http://www.natsar.org/ndwm2.htm
National Search and Rescue, San Francisco, CA

http://www.wxsystems.com
Weather Systems Co., Santa Clara, CA

http://www.skyview.co.uk/weather.html
Skyview Systems Co., Sudbury, England

http://www.robertwhite.com/index.html
Robert E. White Instruments, Boston, MA

http://www.rainwise.com
RainWise, Inc., Bar Harbor, ME

http://www.americanweather.com
American Weather Enterprises, San Francisco, CA

Weather Software

http://cirrus.sprl.umich.edu/wxnet/software.html

The WeatherNet site at the University of Michigan has a very large selection of downloadable software and shareware for either PC or Macintosh computers. You can download weather conversion software, data analysis software, weather camera software, weather station software, gridding software, and numerous others. Most of the software is free. Before downloading anything from the Internet, get your parents' permission.

Weather Radio

Every successful weather watcher should also own a weather radio. Weather radios are available at Radio Shack and similar stores. They usually range in price from ten to fifty dollars.

Weather Organizations

The American Meteorological Society is the largest and most complete professional organization for people in the fields of weather and climate. Through AMS, weather watchers, weather weenies, and weather professionals can find the latest publications and booklets on weather and climate, information on careers in weather or meteorology, information on scholarships, local AMS chapter directories, and many other useful resources. The AMS website is at

http://www.ametsoc.org/AMS/